Instructing
a Child's Heart

Instructing
a Child's Heart

TEDD & MARGY TRIPP

Shepherd Press
Wapwallopen, Pennsylvania

Instructing a Child's Heart
©2008 by Tedd Tripp and Margy Tripp
ISBN 978-0-9815400-0-9

Unless otherwise indicated, all Scripture quotations taken from the HOLY BIBLE, NEW INTERNATIONAL VERSION®. Copyright © 1973, 1978, 1984 International Bible Society. Used by permission of Zondervan. All rights reserved.

Italics or bold text within Scripture quotations indicate emphasis added.

Page design and typesetting by Lakeside Design Plus
Cover design by Tobias' Outerwear for Books

First Printing, 2008
Printed in the United States of America

RRD 18 17 16 15 14 13 12
     13 12 11 10   9   8   7   6

Dedicated to the memory of Margy's parents
Reverend Carl R. Ellenberger (1919–2000)
and to Mrs. Eva Ellenberger (1919–),
whose dedicated service to Christ
and constant prayer for their
children, grandchildren,
and great grandchildren
exemplify the spirit and message of this book

Contents

Preface

How critical is it to provide your children with a worldview that gives them a framework to understand your instruction and discipline? You may be surprised that this book is titled *Instructing a Child's Heart*. You may ask, "Why not title the book *Instructing a Child's Mind*? Isn't instruction directed to the mind?"

The Importance of the Heart

We often think of the mind as the reasoning aspect and the heart as the emotional part of a person. The Bible does not support that idea. The Bible links thought to the heart. When God sent the Great Flood it was because "every inclination of the thoughts of [man's] heart was only evil all the time" (Gen. 6:5). Mary, the mother of Jesus, finding herself overwhelmed with all she had heard concerning her son, "treasured up all these things and pondered them in her heart" (Lk. 2:19). The power of the word of God is seen in the way "it judges the thoughts and attitudes of the heart" (Heb. 4:12).

The Bible ascribes reasoning and thinking to the heart because the heart is the center of one's being. The heart is where we think, grieve, rejoice, love, hate, desire, fear, pray, and so forth. "The heart is the wellspring of life" (Prov. 4:23).

The Importance of Instruction

Instructing a child's heart is not simply transferring data from parent to child. It is impressing the heart with truth. Solomon gives this kind of instruction when he says, "My son, if your heart is wise, then my heart will be glad; my inmost being will rejoice when your lips speak what is right. Do not let your heart envy sinners, but always be zealous for the fear of the LORD. There is surely a future hope for you, and your hope will not be cut off. Listen, my son, and be wise, and keep your heart on the right path" (Prov. 23:15–19). Solomon appeals to his son's heart.

Expectations of a Child Rearing Book

Moms and dads are looking for tips and ideas that have immediate application to their children. Parents have a "top ten" list of problems they would like to know how to solve. Parents want practical help, "Just tell me what to do when. . . , or tell me what to say when . . ."

You need more than tips and ideas; you need solid biblical truth. Even if we could script conversations and put well-chosen words into your mouth, it would not meet your needs. You would quickly get beyond our script and run out of words. Each interaction within a family has its own unique set of circumstances and personalities. Because God has made human beings and their world complex, there aren't simple formulas that can be applied to our parenting. If all you have are tips and strategies, you will get beyond your fund of knowledge. Your greatest need is to understand deep truths from the Bible. Solid parenting skills are built on solid truth.

Organization of the Book

We have organized this book into three major sections. The first looks at the call to formative instruction. This portion looks at formative instruction with a wide lens. In the second section we zero in on more specific topics. The truths discussed in this section must be the substance of formative instruction for your child. It will include chapters on the importance of the heart, sowing and reaping, God's plan for authority, the glory of God, wisdom and foolishness, how we are complete in Christ and the importance of the church. This is lifesaving formative instruction.

The third section focuses on the application of formative instruction. Practical "how to" instruction for correction, discipline and motivation will help make the connection between formative instruction and corrective discipline. This section will include chapters on subjects such as consequences, getting from behavior to the heart and communication basics for corrective discipline. All corrective interventions must focus on the good news of the gospel. We want our children to see the forgiving, tranforming, empowering grace of Jesus Christ in the gospel.

Instructing a child's heart is essential to shepherding a child's heart. The instruction that you provide not only informs the mind; it is directed to persuading the heart of the wisdom and truthfulness of God's ways. We should impress truth on the hearts of our children, not to control or manage them, but to point them to the greatest joy and happiness that they can experience—delighting in God and the goodness of his ways.

Margy and Tedd Tripp
August 2006

PART ONE

The Call to Formative Instruction

CHAPTER 1

Life Is a Classroom

Life is a classroom. It truly is. Teaching and learning are in process twenty-four hours a day. Here's the danger! In the absence of biblical formative instruction, secular formative instructors take over. Our hearts are easily captivated by the hollow and deceptive philosophies of a godless culture (Col. 2:8). The majority culture interprets life *worldview* through unregenerate eyes and promotes its conclusions through various means, from advertising to education. It is like the air you breathe; you breathe it in without noticing it! So do your children! The formative instruction of our secular culture is a frightening reality. How can parents compete with the world for the minds and hearts of their children?

Two Fundamental Answers

First, we must identify the enemy and acknowledge his troop strength *identify the enemy* (see 1 Pet. 5:8). I use a war analogy because God says we're engaged in a battle (Eph. 6:11–12). The battle is inside us (Jas. 4:1) and outside of us (Eph. 6:12). Christians must take time to identify their spiritual enemies and to assess the enemy's power and influence. Failure to do so places us in spiritual peril. Often, sincere Christians feed and house the enemy (the secular culture) and feel they can somehow contain its influence on their family. They realize too late the pronouncement of James 4:4 that, "Friendship with the world is hatred toward God," and, "Anyone who chooses to be a friend of the world becomes an enemy of God." We cannot invite the secular culture into our homes and expect its voice not to be compelling to us or our children.

Second, we must become skilled at using biblical formative instruction as an offensive and defensive weapon against the enemy of our children's souls (Eph. 6:10–17 and 1 Pet. 5:8). We are responsible to guard our children against the wicked formative instruction of the world. Formative instruction gives children principles and absolutes by which to live—hooks to hang life on. Will they be our hooks or the majority culture's hooks?

In Proverbs Solomon repeatedly warned his sons to avoid bad counsel and to take his wise counsel. His teaching has two aspects. First he expounded on the danger of following the example of the ungodly. "My son, when sinners entice you . . ." (Prov. 1:10). Then he encourages his sons to pursue the path of life. "Let the wise listen, and add to their learning" (Prov. 1:5). In this chapter, we will begin by looking at the constant formative instruction of the secular culture. Secular culture is powerful and cannot be quarantined. We must understand the overwhelming shaping force of secular culture in order to undertake formative instruction. Romans 12:2 gives us a good outline. Identify the enemy. "Do not conform any longer to the pattern of this world, but be transformed by the renewing of your mind." Provide biblical formative instruction. "Then you will be able to test and approve what God's will is—his good, pleasing and perfect will."

The glorious reality is this—As we battle, we are assured of eternal victory because of a Savior who has already vanquished the foe. Our faltering but determined and confident use of his battle strategy and weaponry will win the day (1 Cor. 15:57–58 and 1 Pet. 5:9–10).

Identify the Enemy

Who Instructs in Our Majority Culture?

The secular culture we live in understands the need to saturate us with its message. Let's consider these powerful mediators of values. Celebrities from every entertainment medium tell us how to act. "Experts" instruct us about how to live, regardless of our interest or need. Electronic media socializes our culture. Television, cinema, the print media and cyberspace broadcast their values. It's tailor-made for each generation—whether you're two, twelve, thirty-two, or sixty-five. The advertisers know what appeals to their target audience!

Advertisers repeat their message. They know that it will take more than one exposure for their message to be absorbed. If it didn't need repetition, they would create quick and inexpensive ads that aired only once. Advertisers want you to memorize their jingles so that you remember them when you are facing the wall of available products, trying to decide which one to buy! The world gets it! Shaping ideas requires long-term interaction with long-range goals and 100 percent saturation.

What do They Teach?

It's the same message for every generation—but slickly tailored to the hot buttons of each. The underlying message is ME! I deserve . . . , *it's all about Me* I want . . . , I will be happy if . . . , I can't live without . . . These messengers tell us and our children how to think about life, themselves, other people and God.

Talk show entertainers schmooze adults into emotional and unprincipled views of everything from relationships to ethics. Affluence, self-indulgence, and physical, emotional and financial security are promoted as the right and privilege of the mature. Advertising whets our appetite for the ease and comforts we crave and "plastic" opens the door to ownership.

The majority culture has taught our children that authority and traditional values are repulsive. With each generation, children demand bigger incentives to cooperate with authority. Sports heroes and movie stars underscore the message. Advertising offers meaning, identity and pleasure through clothing, new experiences, cars and "stuff."

All the material things huckstered by the world give our children inordinate sensual appetites that can never satisfy creatures who were created for God. These inordinate appetites cheapen their experience of life and lead them away from God.

I was recently talking to a Russian woman who showed me a picture of her daughter in Belarus. She was wearing tight blue jeans and a vest with a bare midriff. She would pass for any cool American teenager. Why? Because the same culture-shapers sell in Belarus as in any American city—and the culture-shapers are strong. They cross all boundaries of geography and language.

Ironically, cynicism reigns in the majority culture. Adults are cynical because their expectations of a successful life have long since been dashed. Even the few who are "successful" have found it an empty prize. Young people are cynical because their raw and savvy culture leaves them with no transcendent values, only survival by whatever means serves their lusts and desires for the moment! They are depressed, restless, critical, argumentative, unmotivated and unimpressed with previous generations' successes.

The World's Classroom Is Deceptive

The classroom of modern life is the comfortable sofa in the TV room, the iPod, the CD player and headset, the magazines in the dentist's office, the car radio, the billboards, the workplace, the Little League field or dance studio. And the teachers are skilled in crafting the message to be entertaining, reasonable, appealing and tailor-made for us and our children. Their curriculum is sophisticated, persuasive and tactile—bent on engaging the idol factories of our hearts.

Does this sound too dramatic or overstated? Look at Psalm 1. God warns us with an evaluation of the worldly culture. The Psalmist used the "walk, stand, sit" metaphors to describe our unwitting presence in a daily, godless classroom. The "counsel of the wicked," "the way of sinners" and "the seat of mockers" identify the teachers and their methods and message. Verses 4 to 6 declare their sad end. "They are like chaff that the wind blows away. Therefore the wicked will not stand in the judgment, nor sinners in the assembly of the righteous. . . . the way of the wicked will perish."

Provide Biblical Formative Instruction

The Importance of Parental Formative Instruction

The life classroom is constant, compelling and comprehensive. The same is true of our homes as well. They are environments where our children are constantly learning.

Not only that, but we are always teaching our children. Our every response, whether it is instruction or silence, teaches. Our behavior and our love teach. But in addition to that natural process, God calls us to instruct our children about what to believe, how to think from the Scriptures, and how to live. In this book we will call that deliberate teaching "formative instruction." Formative instruction "forms" or "shapes" our children. It is not a single event, but a lifetime of interaction that is based on God's revelation. We are promised that our teaching will bear fruit in our children's lives (Prov. 22:6).

We must actively teach our children, and live the reality, that God defines life. He tells and shows us the truth about what is valuable, what is worth living and dying for, what is worth doing and being, and what gives our lives significance. Rather than simply fixing short-term problems, we parents must have a vision for formative instruction from infancy to adulthood.

teach it, live it; God defines life

These realities are summed up in Matthew 22:37–39: "Love the Lord your God with all your heart and with all your soul and with all your mind. . . . Love your neighbor as yourself." What does that love for God and others look and sound like? Where do I find wisdom, direction, stamina and the ability to overcome my sinful nature, and to love God and others? The answer is in God's revelation—his instruction to man. The Bible is our curriculum for formative instruction. Christ is our example of how to live the Bible.

What do I substitute for it?

God Has Spoken

God's Word teaches us how to understand all human knowledge and experience in the light of his existence and his involvement in our world. This sets biblical instruction apart from both the immoral perversion of the modern day and the humanistic worldview that is traditional, time-honored and well-heeled.

Our objective when we teach our children is not simply to ensure, by some venerable or socially accepted child rearing method, that our children are not criminals, or that they "do well." Rather, our desire is that they should love the Lord their God with all their heart, soul and mind. Therefore, formative instruction must be rooted in Scripture, not in what Dr. Phil and Dr. Laura advise, or what *Parents* magazine recommends or even what the pediatrician tells us to do.

the GOAL!

Parents Must Speak

As parents, it is our divinely appointed task to commend God's works to the next generation (Ps. 145:4). We are to proclaim God's truth—not our own ideas. We get a sense of the importance of God's words in Deuteronomy 32:46–47, "Take to heart all the words I have solemnly declared to you this day, so that you may command your children to obey carefully all the words of this law. . . . They are not just idle words for you—*they are your life*" (emphasis author's).

The Scriptures teach repeatedly that God's Word alone provides truth that can bring life to the hearer. Our words must echo this. But they must not only echo word for word. A mere echo could have a hollow ring, as it did for the Pharisees. These life-giving words must be processed, applied and taught with love, so that our children learn how to put that word into practice in their circumstances. Scripture teaches that parents' words carry weight because they are messengers of the living God. Our very lives express God's Word as well. Christ's physical presence in our world showed us what God was like, because Christ said, "He who has seen me has seen the Father" (Jn. 14:9). When we speak and live the words of God, we too speak and live with authority (see 1 Pet. 4:11).

not just an echo

> Many parents feel like they are victims of hostile and alien forces that have invaded their homes through MTV, VH1, video game hardware and software. Their children have interests, a vocabulary, and values—an entire culture that they, the parents, know nothing about.
>
> I have asked concerned parents, "How did your child afford a video game, a TV, and computer for their bedroom?"
>
> "Oh, he didn't buy it; I bought it for him."
>
> "You bought it for him and now you are upset with him because he uses it?"
>
> We must be discerning about the entertainment we provide. We may be inviting unwelcome guests who become difficult to evict.

Honor for God, respect for authority, respect for others, and a gracious and productive atmosphere in our homes will be some of the blessings of biblical formative instruction. Modern homes can be the shelter where dignity, loyalty to family values and standards are kept, helping our children to face the world and its challenges each day. Parenting is not just child-care. We can have a vision for formative instruction that will transform our homes and communities.

Formative Instruction and Discipline Are Not the Same Thing

instruction vs discipline

Don't confuse formative instruction with corrective discipline. Formative instruction should be happening all the time. Discipline should be applied only when behavior needs to be corrected. If the only time we *instruct* is when our children need *discipline*, our children will not listen to our instruction for fear of the discipline. They will also interpret discipline through the culture's view of discipline—as abusive, dictatorial, a violation of personal rights, archaic and fanatic.

Our formative instruction must teach that discipline is part of God's essential way for parents to provide protection, direction, safety and blessing to children. Discipline alone is not adequate instruction. Corrective discipline is understood when it is founded on effective biblical formative instruction. Corrective discipline without adequate formative instruction sows seeds of confusion and rebellion in children.

A Treasure—Not a Baseball Bat

Beware! Do not use the Scriptures to beat up your children! "Fathers, do not provoke your children to wrath" (Eph. 6:4). If you beat up your children with God's Word, they will shrink from it when they are young and flee from it when they live independently. We must pay attention to our children and be sensitive to them in order to know when we are beating up our children verbally.

How do you think of the Bible? Is it law, condemnation, warning, guilt, threats and judgment? Or is it God's merciful and gracious revelation for fallen, broken humanity? The Bible provides in God-inspired, rich literary textures, the story of creation, the Fall, the incarnation, redemption and hope through the life and death of Jesus Christ, and a glorious second coming of Jesus to establish the new heavens and the new earth.

We must teach our children to love the Scriptures. We must teach the promises along with the warnings. We must teach the perfect sacrifice of Christ for sin along with the description of our sinfulness. We must let our children hear how God's law is sweeter than honey from the honeycomb. By it we are warned, and by keeping it there is great reward (Ps. 19:10–11). The most effective way to teach our children to love the Scripture is to love it ourselves. They will see us longing to read it, hear it and understand it, and learn that it is valuable.

CHAPTER 2

Five Goals for Formative Instruction

As we engage our children with formative instruction we must have the big picture in mind. The following five perspectives are important to keep in mind as we undertake formative instruction.

- Remember Scripture is our personal history
- Develop godly habits
- Apply Scripture to life
- Model spiritual vitality
- Grow into a mature relationship with your children

Keeping these five perspectives or goals in focus will give energy and shape to our formative instruction.

Scripture Is Our Personal History

In Deuteronomy 6:20–25, Moses challenged the people of Israel to follow God by recalling God's provision. His words carried weight because the Israelites knew their history and the God who revealed himself to Abraham, Isaac, and Jacob. Israel's history rehearsed over and over again who God was and what he had done for them. They read, recited, sang, chanted, and memorized their history. Their dietary laws protected them from the diseases suffered by other nations, so even their foods were reminders of God's covenantal protection and provision. This culture-shaping revelation from God gave Israel clear identity and purpose in the midst of the circumstances they faced.

The same is true for us. God has revealed himself to us in the Scriptures, telling us who we are and why we were created. Scripture is *our* history. Creation, Fall, and Redemption are the context for understanding life. Our children cannot understand why they are in this world, how sin has affected them, and how redemption restores what sin has destroyed, apart from their spiritual history.

Imagine a counselor hearing a counselee's life problems and then charging ahead with advice, before asking questions to understand the background and circumstances of the counselee's life. The counsel given may have good content, but it will lack depth, and lasting help will be elusive. The same is true when we instruct our children without giving them the context of their history.

The Scripture teaches us much about the world we live in. It teaches us that God created the world. The Scripture teaches us about God's people in the past and how God's redemptive promise of Genesis 3:15 has been unfolding over the centuries. But Scripture teaches much more. Scripture is history that tells us about ourselves.

This revelation isn't just about distant physical and spiritual relatives—it's about each of us by name. Let that truth wash over you with all its implications and power. Bathe our children in that truth. Otherwise, the Bible's prophecies, provisions, promises, and pronouncements will not motivate our speech and behavior. And our children will treat the Bible like a news story.

Here's what I mean. We may feel enthused by some act of heroism on the evening news and even remark how great it is to hear that occasional acts of valor still break into this bleak world. But think of the family loyalty inspired by personal attachment to the hero, and the pride and emulation it would engender. The sad and hopeless plight of the starving in a distant land may stir our compassion and create in us a purpose to respond some time by some means. But think of the restlessness and untiring effort we would expend if it was a family member caught in famine or catastrophic misfortune.

What a difference perspective makes! The faith, hope, and confidence of heroes of faith in the Bible and church history are born of personal identity with God's revelation. They saw themselves in God's unfolding story. Christ's glorious kingdom and the struggles of the unseen world of spiritual reality must be as real and urgent to our children and us as the stories gossiped about at our family reunions. The protagonists in the Bible narratives must be as accessible to our minds and hearts as Grandma, Sister Sue, and Uncle Bill. Then who God is and what he has done will be a significant element in our instruction and discipline! We must learn this first in our own lives.

David says in Psalm 34:8–11, "Taste and see that the LORD is good; blessed is the man who takes refuge in him. Fear the LORD, you his saints, for those who fear him lack nothing. The lions may grow weak and hungry, but those who seek the LORD lack no good thing." Then teach it to our children. "Come, my children, listen to me; I will teach you the fear of the LORD." Scripture is not only about God's people of old—it's about us and our children. The Bible is our family album.

> Do you want your children to be bold and courageous? Bring David the shepherd boy to life, facing the lion and the bear as God's preparation for defying Goliath. The story of David is not only a Bible story. It is part of our children's history because David is their older brother in the faith. His courage is a model for our children's courage and faith as they face their battles.

Let me briefly outline our history. The beginning of Genesis describes how God created the universe. Then creation was spoiled by the Fall. Man's only hope for redemption is through God's provision in his Son.

The history books of the Bible underscore and illustrate our need for a Savior. The narratives show God's faithfulness to us. They remind us of the blessings and curses of the covenant. They trace the genealogy of the promised Redeemer. They provide the historical backdrop for the ministry of the prophets.

The books of poetry chronicle vivid personal experiences of knowing God in the context of life's joys, sorrows, troubles, and afflictions. The writers express the fear of the Lord while responding to life's challenges. They contrast wisdom and foolishness and furnish us with the powerful tools for receiving the Word of the Lord and communicating it to our children.

The books of prophecy pronounce judgment on Israel for straying. Woven into the message of judgment is God's plan for deliverance because of his mercy. The prophets powerfully illustrate true repentance and restoration.

The Gospels are dramatic. The life of Christ unfolds all the promises, types, and shadows of the Old Testament and demonstrates the authenticity of God's revelation. He is powerful bringing all things to pass! The Messiah comes in time and space to fulfill all righteousness.

The Epistles interpret and apply the ministry of the Redeemer promised in Genesis 3:15.

Christ is the heart of the Scriptures. He is there as the creative Word in Genesis, and as the exalted Savior in Revelation. Revelation 1 through 20 record God's power in keeping the church safe through persecution. Chapters 21 and 22 prophesy God bringing everything to the glorious end of exalting Christ before the nations, as he brings judgment on all created things and establishes his glorious and eternal kingdom.

We must show our children the vital connection between the powerful story of redemption in the Scriptures and their daily experience. The instruction we give them will only make sense in the context of the story of the Scriptures that tells them who they are and about the God who made them and offers them redemption.

> You and your children live on the continuum between creation and the new heavens and the new earth. Your experience of the sensory world can only be understood and interpreted by its place in God's redemptive history. Only Scripture can make sense of your life experience. Humanism is hollow and unsatisfying in light of biblical truth. Only God's word can bring true comfort. Man's sentimental words are like Band-Aids on gaping wounds. Only the Bible holds lasting counsel that will not disappoint or turn us out of his way. A primary goal in instruction must be to show your children who God is and what he has done—to show them their story in the pages of Scripture. Make the Bible your family album, not someone else's story. The Bible is not about "them" and "then," but "us" and "now."

Teach Children to Develop Godly Habits

The second goal is to teach our children to develop habits of life that reflect truth. Early instruction results in patterns that are resistant to change—whether good or bad! "Train a child in the way he should go, and when he is old he will not turn from it" (Prov. 22:6).

Young children hear and heed instruction that is graciously firm and authoritative, but also fairly represents the boundaries the parents establish. When children live without a clear, consistent presentation of biblical reality, their sinful nature will read and interpret reality for them. Their hearts will cut a path that satisfies their lusts and desires to serve themselves.

Early instruction that interprets life experiences, and challenges heart attitudes and responses with righteous words, prepares the soil of the heart for the plowing of the Holy Spirit. Paul recognizes the power of this process in the life of Timothy. Timothy's spiritual life was tied to early training in the Scriptures described in 2 Timothy 1:5 and 3:14–15:

I have been reminded of your sincere faith, which first lived in your grandmother Lois and in your mother Eunice and, I am persuaded, now lives in you also. But as for you, continue in what you have learned and have become convinced of, because you know those from whom you learned it, and how from infancy you have known the holy Scriptures, which are able to make you wise for salvation through faith in Christ Jesus.

The training qualities of Scripture are richly described in the familiar words of 2 Timothy 3:16–17. "All Scripture is God-breathed and is useful for teaching, rebuking, correcting and training in righteousness, so that the man of God may be thoroughly equipped for every good work."

David's devotion to God as a young man is understood as he describes the path of purity, "How can a young man keep his way pure? By living according to your word. I seek you with all my heart; do not let me stray from your commands. I have hidden your word in my heart that I might not sin against you. Praise be to you, O LORD; teach me your decrees. With my lips I recount all the laws that come from your mouth. I rejoice in following your statutes as one rejoices in great riches. I meditate on your precepts and consider your ways. I delight in your decrees; I will not neglect your word" (Ps. 119:9–16).

You want your children to develop the habit of prayer during times of temptation. Imagine a four-year-old who becomes angry with siblings over every offense, real or imagined. You want to accomplish more than adjudicating the conflict of the day. You want him to turn to God in prayer when he is tempted to be angry.

Have this conversation with him in the morning.

"Today you may be tempted to be angry with your sister. When you are tempted, I want you to come to Mommy and I will help you pray to God for grace. God can help you when you are tempted to be angry."

If your young child can learn to come to you to lead him to the throne of grace to find mercy and help in his time of need (Heb. 4:16), he will learn how to go there himself in the years to come.

Apply Scripture to Everyday Life

Children need instruction to apply Scripture to issues of authority, obedience, conflict resolution, and God-given roles in relationships. Everyday life affords scores of opportunities to connect Scripture to life—from lost book-bags to broken friendships and poor test grades. Scores of training opportunities evaporate without notice as we hurry through our days thinking that devotional time with our children is enough. Our responses to the circumstances and crises of everyday life make our theology real.

Bible stories glow with illustrations of children whose knowledge of Scripture translated into obedient, bold action. David's words to Saul sound naïve and childish in the face of the Philistine army and the terrifying threats of Goliath, "Let no one lose heart on account of this Philistine; your servant will go and fight him" (1 Sam. 17:32). But David's spiritual life and experience as a boy shepherd resounds with his right to speak. "But David said to Saul, 'Your servant has been keeping his father's sheep. When a lion or a bear came and carried off a sheep from the flock, I went after it, struck it and rescued the sheep from its mouth . . . Your servant has killed both the lion and the bear . . . The LORD who delivered me from the paw of the lion and the paw of the bear will deliver me from the hand of this Philistine'" (1 Sam. 17:34–37).

David's courageous speech to Saul and the ensuing challenge to Goliath did not spring from foolhardy boyhood fantasy. David believed in God's power and authority. The God who brought Israel out of Egypt was the same God who delivered him from the bear and the lion. His confidence came from facing the bear, crying out to God for help, and knowing God's deliverance. Saul looked at Goliath and Goliath looked big; God and his promises looked small. David looked at Goliath and the Philistine horde with the history of Israel and his own dangerous encounters looming in his mind. He applied what he knew to be true about God and his promises. As a result, God looked big beside the finite and earthbound giant. "You come against me with sword and spear and javelin, but I come against you in the name of the LORD Almighty, the God of the armies of Israel, whom you have defied. This day the LORD will hand you over to me . . . All those gathered here will know that it is not by sword or spear that the LORD saves; for the battle is the Lord's, and he will give all of you into our hands" (1 Sam. 17:45–47).

Model Spiritual Vitality for Our Children

The surest way to teach children to apply God's truth to life's circumstances is to model it for them. Parenting that exhibits a vital *Model it* relationship with God in all the joys and storms of life is irresistible to children and young people. Conversely, the surest way to harden our children's hearts to God and his ways is "having a form of godliness but denying its power" (2 Tim. 3:5).

Our homes are the laboratory of life for our children. They will believe that Christian faith is the genuine article if we *know* God—not just know about God. As children grow to young adulthood in our churches, they are searching desperately for a faith that has the warmth and vitality of close relationship with the living God, and the sure footing of sound doctrine that will stand the storms of life. Relationship with God is the passionate assurance that the Sovereign God of the Bible can be known by his people in all the experiences of life. Our relationship with God will beckon our children to draw near to him as their source of comfort and rest.

> Recount for your children the Bible stories of other young people who applied scriptural truth to the events in their lives. Shadrach, Meshach, Abednego (Dan. 3); Daniel (Dan. 1:8-21; ch. 6); Esther; the little servant girl in Naaman's house (2 Kings 5:1-15); and Miriam, as she approached Pharaoh's daughter (Ex. 2)—all these young people had courage and conviction because of training in the Scriptures. They applied the truth they had recited and sung about to the events in their lives, and that truth dictated their choices.

Grow into a Mature Relationship with Your Children

Strive to grow into a mutual relationship of living and working together for Christ's kingdom. The Christian life is lived in a community. Throughout redemptive history God's people have witnessed God's awesome deeds and gloried together in his protection and provision. Future generations are also in view. We must have the same sense of expectation as we talk of God's faithfulness and provision for our physical family and our spiritual family—that we will work together to proclaim Christ's kingdom until he comes. Joshua declares this expectation in chapter 24:15, "But as for me and my household, we will serve the LORD."

The same themes are in the Psalms. Psalm 48:12–14 tells us, "Walk about Zion, go around her, count her towers, consider well her ramparts, view her citadels, that you may tell of them to the next generation. For this God is our God for ever and ever; he will be our guide even to the end."

Psalm 78:3–7 reminds us, "What our fathers have told us. We will not hide them from their children; we will tell the next generation the praiseworthy deeds of the LORD, his power, and the wonders he has done. He decreed statutes for Jacob and established the law in Israel, which he commanded our forefathers to teach their children, so the next generation would know them, even the children yet to be born, and they in turn would tell their children. Then they would put their trust in God and would not forget his deeds but would keep his commands."

In the next chapter we will examine the primary template in the Bible for understanding this calling—Deuteronomy 6.

CHAPTER 3

The Call to Formative Instruction

We were on a family vacation in California. My four-year-old son and I were in a boat going through Disneyland's "Pirates of the Caribbean" amusement ride. As bombs appeared to be exploding and water was splashing all around us, he turned to me and asked, "Daddy, is this real or is this pretend?" He was doing a reality check. "If this is real I'm going to be scared to death. If it is just pretend, I can relax and enjoy the ride."

Interpreting reality for our children is important. The call to formative instruction is a call to provide our children with a grid for interpreting and responding to reality.

Definition of Formative Instruction

Formative instruction is teaching that "forms" our children. It enables them to root life in God's revelation in the Bible. It provides a culture for our children, a culture that is distinctly Christian. It shows our children the glory and excellence of God. It helps them understand the dignity of mankind as God's image bearers. It provides a way of interpreting life through the redemptive story of God, who reconciles people to himself.

Formative instruction is "before the problem" instruction. Its focus is interpreting and responding to life in biblical ways. It is both planned and unplanned. Family worship, for example, is planned to bring rich biblical truth to our children. But there are also many unplanned opportunities for formative instruction in the ebb and flow of daily living. As life catches us unexpectedly, our responses are formative instruction

Culture in this context means the integrated pattern of knowledge, belief, and behavior that underlies our interpretation of our experience. The "knowledge and belief" aspects of the culture we provide for our children helps answer the question, "Why do we...?" It explains the norms and standards of behavior. At the same time, the norms and standards of behavior that we hold out for our children reinforce and embody the pattern of knowledge and belief we teach them. We use good table manners because we believe that we should show respect to others, and pleasant manners is a way to show respect. At the same time, the fact that we use and expect good table manners reinforces for our children the belief that the people they're eating with should be treated with respect and courtesy.

for our children. Our faith in God in the face of trials, our love and compassion for others, our forgiving and kind spirit, our confidence in the power of the gospel, our hope in grace—all breathe life into our formative instruction.

Recently, we observed a wonderful illustration of unplanned instruction. A young father was helping his three-year-old son respond to being bowled over and losing a toy to a more aggressive child during some chaotic play at a social gathering. This dad rescued his son with kind words.

"It's okay, Jordan, you can let him have the toy. There are a lot of other toys here to play with." The son was reluctant to respond to this suggestion of kindness.

"It is hard to be kind sometimes, isn't it?" the dad continued.

"Yes," his son nodded, his lower lip quivering.

"Who can help you be kind?" the father inquired.

"Jesus."

"That's right, Jesus can help you. Let's pray and ask Jesus for help."

This was a powerful example of unplanned formative instruction. This father was presenting a culture to his son. This conversation modeled kindness and forgiveness. It modeled humble dependence on Christ for grace and enablement.

Problem of Assuming Too Much

Often our formative instruction is inadequate or incomplete because we make massive assumptions about what our children understand.

We sent our young son off to camp. Margy, of course, packed his things. She put a week's worth of mothering in the suitcase. During a guided tour of the suitcase, she said as she showed him his underwear, "Remember, Honey, to put on a clean pair of underpants everyday."

He arrived home a week later looking a little bulky. We soon discovered he was wearing seven pairs of underpants! He had put on a clean pair of underpants every day just as Mother had told him. Margy assumed he knew he should take off the old pair before he put on a clean pair.

We overestimate what our children understand about life. Because of that, we need to be aware of the importance of formative instruction. Everyday interaction provides many opportunities to teach children how God has structured the world in which we live.

Not the Same as Corrective Discipline

Our times of corrective discipline are not the best context for teaching God's ways to our children. First, we are not in our best form as teachers when something has gone wrong. We're upset. "He should have known better. How many times is he going to do this before he learns?" Even if we are not abusive in our manner or words, we are not the best communicators of truth when things have gone wrong. These will not be our finest teaching moments.

One of our college-age children was using a family car to get to a summer job. One afternoon he came home with the bumper lashed to the back of the car with a chunk of rope. Naturally I was curious.

> In the illustration about Jordan the parents are presenting a Christian culture. Jordan can only understand and respond in a Christian way to this situation based on the truth claims of the Word of God. His father will need to have many conversations in which he provides the Christian basis, or worldview, that enables his son to interpret and respond to life according to truth. If the father avoided formative instruction of this sort until Jordan was fifteen years old, he couldn't expect the conversation to make any sense to his son.

"What happened to the car?"

"The bumper fell off."

Notice my son is not the subject, the bumper is. My son is only present here as an observer!

It seems that he dropped a pencil on the floor and drove into a guard rail while he was trying to retrieve it. I did fairly well that night. I was patient and gracious. We had a parts car in the woods; he removed the bumper from both cars in order to make a swap. It got too dark to finish the job that night. So the next day he drove to work without a rear bumper on the car.

That afternoon, he decided to make a k-turn. Making the turn, he backed into the mountain with the bumperless car. When he returned home, not only did the car not have a bumper, the entire trunk was caved in.

As you may imagine, I was not in prime form as a gracious instructor when our car came limping into the drive with the fresh dent. My son needed formative instruction to learn all the lessons that would have protected him from this series of errors. But I was not in my best form as a teacher.

He was also not teachable. He was defensive and self-justifying. So there I stood telling him how foolish he had been. He, meanwhile, was telling me how it really wasn't his fault. It was the pencil's fault, the guard rail's fault, the narrow road's fault. The more he justifies, the more I have to prove he hasn't a leg to stand on. The more I refute, the more he defends. And so it goes.

We never do our best teaching when we are in a discipline situation. Formative instruction—teaching God's ways—must take place apart from the occasions of discipline.

Secondly, if we try to do our formative instruction in the context of corrective discipline, our focus will be too narrow. We will miss the big picture—the opportunity to teach a worldview. We will miss the chance to provide a culture that explains all of life's choices from a distinctly Christian perspective.

Culture answers many questions. What is important? What is valuable? What is worth fighting for? What truth claims are valid? How do those things shape life? How should my relationships be structured? What are the convictions by which I must live? What is entertaining? What is the function of entertainment? How should I think about my appearance?

You simply cannot weave these complex culture issues into every conversation during times of discipline and correction. The particular incidents that you respond to in correction are only illustrative of larger culture issues. They illustrate biblical principles that make up an accurate picture of God's world. Formative instruction is the foundation for corrective discipline; it creates the structure for corrective discipline.

Old Testament Illustration

Joshua 24 is a powerful illustration of the importance of formative instruction. You may be familiar with the well-known family text in Joshua 24, "But as for me and my household, we will serve the LORD" (Josh. 24:15).

Recall the scene. It is Joshua's farewell as a leader of Israel. He reviews God's redemptive acts. He reminds them of God calling Abraham, giving them the land of Canaan, delivering them from Egyptian bondage, and giving them the Promised Land. He reminds them that they live in cities they did not build and eat from vineyards they did not plant. Then Joshua makes his bold declaration that he and his household will serve the Lord. The people respond, "We too will serve the Lord, because he is our God" (Josh. 24:18).

Do you remember what happened? It isn't pretty. The first generation after the conquest of Canaan grew up not knowing the Lord or what he had done for Israel (Judg. 2:10).

How could this happen? How could they not know about the parting of the Red Sea, the manna in the desert, the water God had brought forth from a rock, and the walls of Jericho he caused to fall? What happened? Who failed? Did Joshua fail? Did the priests of Israel fail? Did the prophets in Israel fail?

It was the fathers. The homes and families failed. They failed to do what God called his people to do in Deuteronomy 6.

The Need for Formative Instruction

The primary place for children to receive formative instruction is in the home. Sunday school, VBS, Christian summer camp, Christian school, or even your church's youth programs cannot replace the family. The home is the place where we present a culture that is distinctly Christian.

Our children need a Christian culture. The moral degradation of our society is cultural in its scope. Entertainment, the arts and music, literature, manners, sports, work, leisure, and recreation

God is full of grace and power. He can enable single parents as well as married parents to provide this formative instruction for their children. I have a daughter-in-law who was raised by a single mom who was connected to a strong church. God gave her the grace and insight to raise three children who, now as adults, know and love God.

have all been bent to serve a majority culture that is determined to remove every last vestige of Christian truth from public consciousness. Our children are being told how to think about authority, justice, honor, amusement, responsibility, service, and gender by a culture that has "lost all sensitivity and given itself to sensuality" (Eph. 4:19). The apostle Paul described this in 2 Timothy:

> Avoid choices that make it easy for your children to adopt a youth culture that you know nothing about. Having computers, game devices, TV's and DVD players in children's bedrooms encourages them to develop patterns of thinking that create their own culture distinct from yours. The Christian's endeavor in child rearing is to pass on a culture of value rather than to facilitate independent cultural choices.

> There will be terrible times in the last days. People will be lovers of themselves, lovers of money, boastful, proud, abusive, disobedient to their parents, ungrateful, unholy, without love, unforgiving, slanderous, without self-control, brutal, not lovers of the good.
>
> —2 Timothy 3:1–3

We are raising children in a dangerous culture that is impossible to quarantine. It seeps into our homes through cracks. The electronic game and entertainment industry offers a toxic culture to our children. If we are not self-consciously providing a culture rooted in truth, our children will be more influenced by the majority culture than they are by us and God's truth.

The Call to Formative Instruction

God calls parents to formative instruction in Deuteronomy 6:

> These are the commands, decrees, and laws the LORD your God directed me to teach you to observe in the land that you are crossing the Jordan to possess, so that you, your children and their children after them may fear the LORD your God as long as you live by keeping all his decrees and commands that I give you, and so that you may enjoy long life. Hear, O Israel, and be careful to obey so that it may go well with you and that you may increase greatly in a land flowing with milk and honey, just as the LORD, the God of your fathers, promised you. Hear, O Israel: The LORD our God, the LORD is one. Love the LORD your God with all your

heart and with all your soul and with all your strength. These command-ments that I give you today are to be upon your hearts. Impress them on your children. Talk about them when you sit at home and when you walk along the road, when you lie down and when you get up. Tie them as symbols on your hands and bind them on your foreheads. Write them on the doorframes of your houses and on your gates.

—Deuteronomy 6:1–9

The Goal

The goal of formative instruction is so *that we and our children and our grandchildren may fear the Lord and walk in his ways, enjoying a long life.*

There is more at stake than just meeting the needs of the moment or getting a child to jump through our hoops. Simply solving the im-mediate problems will short-circuit our labors. We will be too focused on getting the problem behind us and getting on with life.

Don't think survival—think kingdom! Therefore we must instill a love for God and his ways in a six-year-old. We must delight our children with a taste of the joys of an unseen world. We are building a worldview that is whole and beautiful because we want our children and grandchildren to follow God. Our concern is focused on where our grandchildren will be fifty years from now.

When and Where

Where and when is formative instruction done? Everywhere. All the time. "Talk about [the ways of God] when you sit at home and when you walk along the road, when you lie down and when you get up" (Deut. 6:7).

There are both formal and informal "when you sit at home" times. We gather as a family for a time of worship. All the family members know that this is the time of day when we read God's Word, discuss his truth, and pray together as a family. I had the joy of being raised in a home in which we had family worship every day. I know that we must have missed some days, but it was so much a part of fam-ily life that I have no recollection of a day that did not begin with family worship.

Other "sit at home" times are informal, but just as purposeful in showing our children the beauty and symmetry of God's truth. When we are just "hanging out," or spending family time together, the ways of God, the goodness of God's care and provision, and the soul-satisfying nature of his truth can fill conversation—not in a way that stifles, but so that the fresh breezes of biblical truth are blowing through the house all the time. The entire creation has been crafted to help us gain a better understanding of God and his revelation. Every door is a reminder that Christ is *the* door. Every day that dawns and night that falls is a reminder that God keeps his promises (Gen. 8:22).

There are times of "lying down." We should bring our children's day to a close by reflecting on the blessings and opportunities of the day, asking forgiveness for the sins of the day, and seeking God for pleasant and restful sleep. Bedtime is a poignant time for reflection, meditation, and thankfulness.

There are times of "rising." We should help our children meet each new day with prayer and gratitude. We should embrace afresh each day the challenges of living in a fallen world in ways that bring glory to God. We should anticipate the day that lies ahead. We should think about the temptations which may present themselves to our children, and the opportunities to reinforce the lessons we taught them yesterday. A two-year-old who struggles with crankiness and whining can be encouraged to find hope and help from God before the first temptation to complain (Phil. 2:14–16). Children benefit from ritual in the ways we put them to bed at night and the ways we help them greet a new day.

> Young dads and moms who were not raised with family worship sometimes ask what exactly family worship is. It is simply a scheduled time in each day when the family gathers together to worship God. After the evening meal was the best time for our family. There are at least three essential ingredients to family worship--singing, reading, and praying. There are excellent resources with creative suggestions to help you make this a part of your family life.[1]

Informal instruction takes place *"as you walk along the road,"* or in the modern sense, as we drive along in the van. If the car is full of chattering children, we have the opportunity to shepherd and refocus conversations in ways that encourage loving God and others.

When we are riding alone with just one of our children, we can talk with them. Think about that particular child's needs, strengths, and weaknesses.[2] Talk about life, about how to interact with life's joys and sorrows in ways that reflect the beauty of God's revelation and the magnanimity of his character.

Inquire about things you know this child is excited about or struggling with. If you have no idea, ask. Don't lose these valuable times to National Public Radio, talk radio, or simply to isolation from each other.

I am not speaking of non-stop monologue. Rather, provide an interpretive lens through which your child can learn to see the world. Hold the prism of God's Word up to the light of ordinary living so it is diffused into a rich spectrum of biblical color that dazzles and shows the glory of God in ordinary life.

One evening when we were building our house, we found ourselves racing home in the midst of a thunderstorm. Just as we passed our neighbor's barn, it was struck by lightning. The lightning rods did their work, so no harm was done. But the flash of light dazzled us with its blinding brilliance. We immediately began talking about God who lives in unapproachable light. Remember, God says that the lightning bolts report to him and he sends them on their way (Job 38:35).

God has designed the world to be a place where his glory is revealed. He has made a world with stones and buildings and sand and roads and paths and rivers and seas and boats and clouds and rain and storms and snow and lightning and mountains and deserts and valleys and bears and cubs and snakes and cattle and sheep and trees and grass and flowers and food and water and sleep and sleeplessness and sickness and tears and health and strength and arms and hands and feet and eyes and ears and heads and bodies and life and death. He has done this in order to display his glories to us. Everything in creation leads to God. Every opportunity to talk infuses life with an understanding that the ways and words of God are everything.

We provide formative instruction even through the décor of the house. Moses says, *"Write them* [God's words] *on the doorframes of your houses and on your gates"* (Deut. 6:9). The point here is that a distinctly Christian culture of thought and interactions must permeate family life so that even our homes become part of the message about living joyfully in the light of God's grace and truth.

A friend had an opportunity to design his home. He built a home with large common rooms that provided brightness and space for easy family living. The bedrooms were too small to make them comfortable places to relax, just good places for changing clothes and sleeping. The use of space said, "We are a family—not individuals sharing a common roof." Artwork and decorations can also communicate the glory of God's ways.

Our Love For God Is Essential

Deuteronomy 6 is not about truth being communicated through some disconnected mouthpiece. God's truth must be life for mom and dad if it is to be life for the children. "Hear, O Israel: The LORD our God, the LORD is one. Love the LORD your God with all your heart and with all your soul and with all your strength" (Deut. 6:4–5).

Our love for God is the foundation for anything we have to say. We cannot impress our children with the fame of God's name if we are not impressed with him ourselves. If the truths about God's sovereign power and incredible mercy have melted our hearts and produced a profound love for God, we will impress our children with his awesome glory. If God's Word is dear to us, it will be important to our children. We must be dazzled by God. We cannot give away what we don't have.

Psalm 34 is an excellent commentary on this point. "Taste and see that the LORD is good; blessed is the man who takes refuge in him" (Ps. 34:8). Here is a marvelous description of delight in God. After further exclamation of God's goodness and provision we read, "Come, my children, listen to me; I will teach you the fear of the LORD" (Ps. 34:11). The one who has tasted the goodness of God is able to teach the fear of the Lord.

"These commandments that I give to you today are to be upon your hearts. Impress them on your children" (Deut. 6:6–7). The things we value and treasure most highly are on our hearts. God's ways cannot be just concepts and ideas; they must be our reason for living.

Richard Edwards, grandfather of Jonathan Edwards, was described as one who "in the presence of God, appeared not only to believe but to delight."[3] Many say they believe in God, but too few delight in him. Delighting in God is more persuasive than many words.

Deuteronomy 4:9 warns, "So that you do not forget the things your eyes have seen or let them slip from your heart as long as you live." We must purpose to keep God's mercies before us at all times. God wants the truth about his being, his character, and his awesome acts of redemption to be on the hearts of his people. These commands imply real danger; these things can slip away.

Keeping an Accurate Picture Before Our Children

We must keep God and his mighty redemption before our children. Our intimate, joyful connection with God, our delight in God, our own gratitude for his mercy and kindness is foundational for impressing truth on the hearts of our children. Remember, the foundations of formative instruction are not merely conceptual; they are deeply spiritual.

Helping Them Interpret Life Correctly

When truth about God is our greatest joy, we will help our children interpret life from a biblical perspective.

Truths to impress on our children:

- Life does not consist in the abundance of possessions. It is not found in new jeans, a new iPod, a car, one's abilities, or exciting, heart-pounding experiences.
- We need to walk in wisdom, submit to the goodness of God's way, and turn away from our own agendas.
- A life of prayer and godly counsel is our desire.
- Choices that are principled rather than popular, foregoing immediate gratification for the sake of eternal reward, are the goal.
- God's authority structures are a blessing. For an eight-year-old this means I can trust Mom's decision that I need an eight o'clock bedtime. Demanding my own way when I still need parental guidance short-circuits God's training process.
- Loving parents are a blessing from God. Loyalty to parental instruction is an expression of gratitude to God. The majority culture offers a fraudulent counterfeit by encouraging young people to be loyal to their peers rather than their parents.
- The heart is the wellspring of life. The things children give their hearts to—the hopes, ambitions, desires, dreams, joys, and concerns—will set the course of life.
- Our hearts cannot be trusted (Jer. 17:9). Our hearts will lie to us. Children (and their parents) are easily entrapped and need to be accessible to others for counsel, instruction, and nurture.

- Friendships are for the purpose of glorifying God, encouraging others, showing love and compassion, and gaining encouragement to do what is right.
- There is a sowing and reaping principle in the Bible and we need to develop a harvest mentality. Children who trust and obey God find their heads crowned with wonderful blessings. Of course, this truth cuts both ways. The ten-year-old boy who is lazy about his chores will reap what he is sowing because God will not be mocked.

Each of these issues has a cultural counterpart that is a lie. Our children are confronted with the lies everyday. We must impress these truths on our children.

Finally, formative instruction enables us to provide a redemptive framework for our decision to follow God's ways in our homes. In the following Scripture, Moses anticipated the opportunity every Christian family would face when he told parents how to reply to their children's questions. Our children eventually ask why we organize life around delighting in God and showing his goodness to others:

> When your son asks you, "What is the meaning of the stipulations, decrees and laws the LORD our God has commanded you?" tell him: "We were slaves of Pharaoh in Egypt, but the LORD brought us out of Egypt with a mighty hand . . . he brought us out from there to bring us in and give us the land that he promised on oath to our forefathers."
>
> —Deuteronomy 6:20–23

The question is, "Why do we worship and serve God? Why have we made choices that are so different from those around us?"

Moses answered, "God has brought redemption to our family. We might have been left in Egypt, but God redeemed us. We have made different choices in order to reflect joy in God and loyalty to him. He has been so good to us. What else would we want to do knowing that mankind's deepest joys are found in knowing the loving God?"

The failure of Israel in Judges 2 was directly tied to the failure of Israel to do what God had called them to do in Deuteronomy 6— to provide formative instruction for their children. The result? A generation grew up not knowing the Lord or what he had done for them.

Hope for Us as We Do This

We do not instruct and disciple our children to make them Christians. Only the Spirit of God can do that. Ultimately, our hope is not that we will get it perfectly right. We, like our children, are part of a fallen race. Each day provides fresh reminders of our failures and need for grace. Our hope as we instruct our children is that the gospel is the power of God to salvation for everyone who believes (Rom. 1:16). In God's kind providence, our children are confronted every day with their need for grace to forgive and to empower them to do what is right. Our hope is that the gospel will be the power of God to salvation in their lives as it has been in ours.

Our hope is the gospel

Perhaps this chapter has alerted you to things you have neglected. You may even wonder, "How can I do these things?" Remember, you can only fulfill God's callings to you in the grace and strength of Jesus Christ. Through him you can do all things (Phil. 4:13).

In the next several chapters we will see some of the specific content of the instruction we must provide for our children.

PART TWO

Introduction to Formative Instruction

The Content of Formative Instruction

The next eight chapters of formative instruction are essential building blocks of a biblical worldview. After reviewing three important principles for instruction, we will examine the importance of the heart, sowing and reaping, God's plan for authority, the glory of God, wisdom and foolishness, how we are complete in Christ, and the importance of the church. This is lifesaving formative instruction.

Formative instruction provides biblical ways for children to think about themselves and their world. For example, when we teach our young children not to hit other people, we are providing a standard for behavior. But the reason for not hitting others is more profound than, "It is not nice," or "How would you like it if you were hit by someone?" We teach them that others are made in God's image. Other children have value and dignity. We give our children big truths they will grow into rather than light explanations they will grow out of.

We must think of ourselves as salespeople for truth. Every experience and every conversation is an opportunity to persuade our children of the beauty and symmetry of God's ways. As children mature, our goal is not to maintain control at any cost; it is rather to persuade. Influence and persuasion are always more important than discipline.

CHAPTER 4

Three Principles for Communicating Formative Instruction

How to Share Biblical Concepts with Children so They Understand

Expressions that we commonly use in the church can be difficult for children to understand. When Tedd was a child, he prayed for the missionaries in the "corn fields." Living in the flat expanses of northwestern Ohio, he could relate to "corn fields." When his parents prayed for the "foreign" fields, he translated it to visions of dedicated missionaries wading through rows of corn in pursuit of lost souls. Everyone laughed over the misunderstanding and realized that "foreign" was not a concept easily grasped by a five-year-old.

Parents make the same mistake with spiritual concepts. Words and phrases like justification, sanctification, slavery to sin, dead in sin, alienation from God, leaning on Jesus, life in the Spirit, dependence on Christ, putting sin to death, complete in Christ, faith, drawing near to God, and worship, sound like a mysterious religious language to our children. They guess at the meaning and are bewildered when their attempts fall short.

A five-year-old girl, learning of her mother's serious illness, desperately and emotionally drew a picture of Jesus, striped like a zebra, and delivered it to her mother's hospital room. She remembered the liturgy well, "By his stripes we are healed." And she believed it. But the true meaning eluded her.

Parents expect attitudes and conduct from children that depend heavily on spiritual understanding, but often children do not understand the spiritual content of the expectations. Children grow in their perception of the gospel as they move from a naïve, tactile, and sensory grasp of the world to a more abstract ability to interact with concepts. This is a process; we do not expect adult heads on little children. We need to teach these spiritual concepts in gentle, compelling ways.

Don't Mix Imaginary Stories with True Bible Stories

We watched in horror on one occasion when Jonah's disobedience to God was played out on a Christian school stage as he visited "Mother Goose Land." The Mother Goose characters tried to give him spiritual direction and get him back on the path to Nineveh. Five and six-year-olds left that experience confused about the difference between the supernatural intervention of God in the lives of his people and Mother Goose fiction. We had to untangle the misconception for our young children. Illustrate spiritual concepts for children by other means than popular entertainment characters.

Don't Trivialize the Gospel to be "Relevant"

When we "bring the Bible down to their level," children quickly outgrow their love and wonder at biblical narratives. Children will grow into their understanding as they realize that God's Word is different from all other literature. It is truth. It is life (Deut. 32:45–47).

Help Young Children Relate to Bible Stories in Tactile and Physical Ways

I can remember Tedd standing on the kitchen table to demonstrate Goliath's height and girth. He measured out the length of his spear on the floor and had the children walk the length. He gave the children rocks to hold to get the full impact of the weight Goliath carried with ease in his armor and weapons. Then he showed David's relative size and gear. David's "confidence in God's might and power" took on meaning as wide-eyed children imagined themselves in David's sandals. The next time we encouraged them to "trust in the Lord," it was a phrase that had substance.

I remember setting out from family devotions on a trek. We were Abraham and Sara and family. Tedd said that we would never return, he didn't know where we were going, or what would happen along the way, but that God would give guidance and provision. Our trek illustrated faith to obey God and trust his promise to be with us. This concept can be introduced in a way that awakens childlike faith in a sovereign heavenly Father who superintends the path of his children.

We played out the scene on the plain of Dura as three young Hebrew men stood in the shadow of Nebuchadnezzar's ninety-foot golden image. We imagined the king threatening them with the fiery furnace if they did not bow down. The story illustrated love and loyalty to God, and true biblical courage. We explained that these boys were scared. No doubt their knees were knocking under their robes as they faced violent and powerful Nebuchadnezzar. Their confidence was different than the brawny and self-confident bravery of human confrontation. These men believed that God would save them, but even if he did not, they would not bow down. Eternal reality was more important to them than temporal existence. What an example for children to live for eternity rather than just for the present!

There is an internal dimension to faith that is the Spirit of God working in the heart. We as parents cannot produce that, but we can provide the "formative instruction" necessary for children to make the connections between religious words and their daily reality.

There are foundational concepts that we must fully grasp in order to pass them on to our children. Sometimes we must unlock their meanings, so they are not trapped in "Christian jargon." Other times they are straightforward concepts that require regular application in daily life.

The next few chapters will discuss these important foundational concepts of our faith, and provide some aids for communicating them to our children.

CHAPTER 5

Getting to the Heart of Behavior

Solomon describes the importance of the heart in Proverbs 4:23, *"Above all else, guard your heart, for it is the wellspring of life."* The heart is like an artesian spring. All our hopes, dreams, and desires gush from the heart. Every drive for meaning and significance originates in the heart. Our behavior flows from the heart—it isn't caused by circumstances or other people. The heart, with its passions and desires, is the wellspring of life.

Recently, Radio Shack had a sale on little matchbox-size remote control cars. "What a fun thing for the grandchildren to play with at grandpa's house," I thought. The next week they were all at our house for a family meal. I got the car out and the children began playing with it. Six children, one car; what was this grandfather thinking?

Within a few minutes I observed one of my grandsons following his sister around imploring her, "Emily (names changed to protect the guilty), remember that Jesus says we should share. Remember that we are to do to another as we would have them do to us. You should be kind and give me a turn."

All these statements are true. And he didn't bowl her over and run off with the controller. But even the most superficial observer knows that this four-year-old was not motivated by concern for his sister's spiritual growth. He didn't care about whether her behavior was Christ-like. He was pursuing the desires of his heart.

Every parent has asked, "Why did you do that?" and then were met with a shrug of the shoulders and "I dunno." Children often react without thought and they are not self-conscious about their motives.

The Heart's Actions

We think of the heart as the emotional organ and the mind as the cognitive organ, but the Bible does not support that idea. The decisions and choices we make in life originate with what we love and desire. The Bible refers to this source as the "heart." Therefore, activities we identify as cognitive are activities of the heart. There are over 750 references to the heart in God's Word. The Scriptures tell us that the heart conceals, discerns, instructs, meditates, muses, perceives, plans, plots, ponders, thinks, and weighs. Though we know scientifically that it is the brain that processes and organizes data, it is the heart that directs even those activities.

Worship Activities Spring from the Heart

The heart loves God, prays to God, rejoices in God, turns to God, seeks God, trusts God, and yields to God. "And now, O Israel, what does the LORD your God ask of you, but to fear the LORD your God, to walk in all his ways, to love him, to serve the LORD your God with all your heart and with all your soul" (Deut. 10:12). Moses' question is a great question—what does God want from us? God wants whole-hearted devotion to him.

God wants full devotion

We teach our children the well-known passage from Proverbs 3, "Trust in the LORD with all your heart, and lean not on your own understanding; in all your ways acknowledge him, and he will make your paths straight" (Prov. 3:5–6). Often people say during pastoral counseling, "I am really having trouble trusting God in this situation." I always ask, "Then, whom are you trusting?" When we are not trusting God, we do not cease trusting. We trust something or someone else, perhaps a friend or our own ideas.

We are always trusting in something

Emotional Activities Flow from the Heart

The heart may ache, cherish, desire, despair, or despise. It may grieve, hate, fear, lament, love, lust, rage, resent, sink, tremble, or throb. The promise of the new covenant in the Old Testament is a promise of heart transformation. "I will give them an undivided heart and put a new spirit in them; I will remove from them their heart of stone and give them a heart of flesh. Then they will follow my decrees and be careful to obey my laws. They will be my people, and I will be their God" (Ezek. 11:19–20).

With the heart we boast, crave, faint, forgive, give, or harbor. The heart may pound, respond, slander, steal, or stray.

The Heart Is What Makes the Person Who They Are

Remember the story of Samuel going to Bethlehem to anoint a new king over Israel? Jesse's son, Eliab, is brought before the prophet. He is a tall, handsome man with a regal bearing. He looks like a man that brave men would follow into battle. Samuel thinks, *"Surely the Lord's anointed stands here before the Lord"*(1 Sam. 16:6). God speaks to Samuel.

"Do not consider his appearance or his height, for I have rejected him. The Lord does not look at the things man looks at. Man looks at the outward appearance, but the Lord looks at the heart" (1 Sam. 16:7). Like Samuel, we become focused on outward appearance. We devote a great deal of time to the outer man, but God is concerned with the heart. Our children will never interpret life correctly until they understand that it is the heart that directs all of life.

The adjectives used in the Bible to describe the heart are an eye-opener. The heart is variously described as adulterous, anguished, arrogant, astray, bitter, blameless, blighted, broken, calloused, circumcised, contrite, crushed, darkened, deadened, deceitful, deluded, devoted, disloyal, envious, evil, faint, faithful, far off, fearful, foolish, grateful, happy, hard, haughty, humble, mad, malicious, obstinate, perverse, proud, pure, rebellious, rejoicing, responsive, righteous, sick, sincere, sinful, steadfast, troubled, unfeeling, uncircumcised, upright, unsearchable, weary, wicked, wise, and wounded. No wonder the Bible says that it is out of the overflow of the heart that the mouth speaks.

The Heart Is Emphasized in Jesus' Ministry

The heart is a major emphasis in the ministry of the Lord Jesus Christ. In the Sermon on the Mount, the Beatitudes describe the primacy of the heart. "Blessed are the pure in heart, for they will see God" (Matt. 5:8).

Whatever we treasure owns our hearts. "For where your treasure is, there your heart will be also" (Matt. 6:21).

Jesus said in Matthew 5:20, "For I tell you that unless your righteousness surpasses that of the Pharisees and the teachers of the law, you will certainly not enter the kingdom of heaven." The Pharisees excelled in performance righteousness. But Jesus is concerned with the heart.

Murder is not simply an external matter. "But I tell you that anyone who is angry with his brother will be subject to judgment . . . Anyone who says, 'You fool!' will be in danger of the fire of hell" (Matt. 5:22).

When Jesus speaks of the sin of adultery, he shows that the commandment is broken by lust. "I tell you that anyone who looks at a woman lustfully has already committed adultery with her in his heart" (Matt. 5:28). In all his teaching, Jesus shows the importance of the heart.

In Matthew 15, the Pharisees accuse Jesus' disciples of defiling themselves by eating with ceremonially unclean hands. Rebuking them, Jesus says, "These people honor me with their lips, but their hearts are far from me. They worship me in vain; their teachings are but rules taught by men" (Matt. 15:8–9).

Children and the Centrality of the Heart

Children who understand the heart understand themselves and others. "For from within, out of men's (children's) hearts, come evil thoughts, sexual immorality, theft, murder, adultery, greed, malice, deceit, lewdness, envy, slander, arrogance, and folly. All these evils come from inside and make a man (child) 'unclean'" (Mk. 7:21–23). We see these things in our children.

Do you ever see greediness at your house? Especially if the candy is being given out! What about deceit? Isn't it amazing how children can mislead you with words that are technically true?

"Did you remember your book bag?"

"Yeah."

"Please get it for me. Let's see if you have any homework to do."

"I can't, I left it in my locker at school."

"I thought you said you remembered it."

"I did remember it. In the bus on the way home I thought, 'Oh, no, I left my book bag at school.'"

This child understood the intent of the question. Yet he answered in a manner that was technically true, but cleverly designed to create an impression that was false.

What about envy? Do you ever see envy at your house? "It's not fair, Dad. He went to Wal-Mart with you three times and I only went to Wal-Mart with you once. It's not fair."

What about slander? My children used to come to me with slander against each other.

"Daddy, brother is being unkind to me . . ."

"Why are you telling me this? Would you like for us to pray for your brother? I am sure he would benefit from our prayers. Or do you want me to scold him?"

Evil thoughts, theft, malice, lewdness, arrogance, and folly; we see it all in our children from time to time. We ask one another, "Where does he get this stuff from?" The Bible tells us it comes from the heart.

The Proper Way to Deal with Children's Hearts

In Luke 6, Jesus uses a tree analogy. "No good tree bears bad fruit, nor does a bad tree bear good fruit" (Lk. 6:43). The ultimate test of a tree is its fruit. Good fruit, good tree. Bad fruit, bad tree. Jesus continues, "Each tree is recognized by its own fruit. People don't pick figs from thornbushes or grapes from briers" (Lk. 6:44).

Fruit reveals the heart.

Now listen to Jesus' application of this truth. "The good man brings good things out of the good stored up in his heart, and the evil man brings evil things out of the evil stored up in his heart. For out of the overflow of his heart his mouth speaks" (Lk. 6:45).

My brother Paul uses the following illustration:

Pretend I have an apple tree in my back yard. Each year it buds and grows apples, but when the apples mature, they are dry, wrinkled, brown and pulpy. After several years I decide it is silly to have an apple tree and never be able to eat its fruit. So I decide that I must do something to "fix" the tree. One Saturday afternoon you look out your window to see me carrying branch cutters, a staple gun, a stepladder, and two bushels of Red Delicious apples into my backyard. You watch carefully as I cut off all the bad apples and staple beautiful red apples onto the branches of the tree. You come out and ask me what I am doing and I say proudly, "I've finally fixed my apple tree."[4]

That is a good example for what we attempt to do with our children. We focus on behavior and lose sight of the attitudes of heart behind the behavior. We try to fix the apples of behavior instead of addressing the serious problem with the tree itself.

don't focus on behavior

Let's suppose my children are fighting over the toys. How am I going to solve this? For the moment I forget all about heart issues and focus on changing the behavior.

"Okay, who had it first?"

Think about this question. It rewards the child who had the toy and ignores the selfishness that is welling up in the hearts of both children. Where in the Bible does it say that the child who had it first is absolved of all responsibility to be a peacemaker? To ask who had it first may solve the fight for the moment, but it does not address the compulsive self-interest of these children who are fighting over the toy.

Or you might bribe your children. "You know, you have fifteen stickers on the refrigerator; when you get five more stickers we are going for ice cream. You could get five stickers today if you are really good." On the other hand, you might threaten your children with punishment.

These are all attempts to control and constrain behavior without addressing the heart. They are attempts to produce godly behavior from a polluted fountain. The child who is not willing to share his toys is reflecting a heart that has strayed. At the very least the fight over the toys displays a love of self.

Return for a moment to the apple tree illustration. What will happen to the apples that I stapled to the tree? They will rot because they are not connected to the life-giving juices of the tree. We may secure the appropriate behavior of our children for the moment through behaviorism, but eventually that behavior will revert to the most natural expression of the abundance of the heart.

> A wonderful Bible study activity with children would be to create a notebook filled with biblical truths about the heart. Children need to have these truths at hand. If you have school-aged children, get them a spiral notebook, do some scrapbooking on the cover of your heart notebook, and fill it with truths about the heart.

Let's imagine that we are able, through behaviorism, to produce appropriate behavior without challenging the ungodly attitudes of heart behind the ungodly behavior. What do we call that sort of change? Isn't that precisely what Jesus condemned in the Pharisees? "You clean the outside of the cup and dish, but inside they are full of greed and self-indulgence... You are like whitewashed tombs, which look beautiful on the outside but on the inside are full of dead men's bones and everything unclean" (Matt. 23:25, 27).

Sandwiched between these two illustrations are Christ's incredibly insightful words, "Blind Pharisee! First clean the inside of the cup and dish, and then the outside also will be clean" (Matt. 23:26). Jesus says behavior will follow the heart. The Pharisees were externalists. Jesus said of them, "Everything they do is done for men to see" (Matt. 23:5).

The Bible provides us with all the categories needed to help our children understand the importance of their hearts. This understanding will make them self-conscious of motivational issues, and they will understand their need for grace.

The Heart's Motives

when : the circumstances
what : what we do or say
why : the motive

Understanding the Heart's Motivations

As we've already seen, the heart is the seat of motivation. Think about it in this way. Behavior has a *when*, a *what*, and a *why*. The *when* of behavior is the circumstance for the behavior. The *what* of behavior are things that one does or says. The *why* of behavior is the motive.

Imagine that I arrive home and find a bike in the driveway. I have to get out of the car and move the bike. Irritated, I go inside to find the child who belongs to the bike.

Imagine at this moment that you, the reader, come along and ask, "Tedd, why are you so angry?" I will probably say, "I am angry because he left his bike in the driveway. This child never listens to me."

But the bike in the driveway is not *why* I am angry, it is *when*. The *when* of my behavior is the circumstance. The *what* of my behavior is my angry outburst. The *why* of my anger is the internal motivation—my attitude of heart. I hate inconvenience. The *why* of my behavior is that I want my will to be done on earth as God's will is done in heaven!

James 4 gives us a wonderful example of all this, "What causes fights and quarrels among you? Don't they come from your desires that battle within you? You want something but don't get it" (Jas.

4:1–2). Fights and quarrels don't come from lack of skill in conflict resolution. They don't come from people who are irritating. They come from desires that battle within. My desires are occupying the place of command and control inside my heart.

Behavior Begins with the Heart

Our desires are not necessarily bad. It is not bad for a father to want his son to park his bike away from the driveway. But that can become an inordinate desire. If I am unkind and unloving because of my desires, then they are inordinate desires.

The Bible gives us many descriptive terms to capture the motives of the heart. Formative instruction helps our children understand that behavior comes from heart attitudes. Teach your children that ungodly behavior begins with ungodly attitudes of heart, but godly behavior begins with godly attitudes of heart. Below is a suggestive list of ungodly heart attitudes and their corresponding godly alternatives.

Ungodly Attitudes	Godly Attitudes
desire for revenge	entrusting self to God
fear of man	fear of God
pride	humility
love of self	love of others
self-preservation	laying down life
fear	perfect love
covetousness	generosity
envy	open-heartedness
hatred	love
anger	forgiveness
desire to be approved by people	desire to be approved by God
anxiety & fear	peace & contentment
rebellion	submission[5]

These lists are not exhaustive, but suggestive of ways the Bible identifies heart attitudes. These motivational attitudes of the heart are the reasons that our children have conflicts with one another. Parents are tempted to short-circuit to behavior management and forget the heart, though the primary issue *is* the heart. To recap—the circumstance is the *when*; behavior is the *what*; attitude of the heart is the *why*.

The Heart's Need for Grace

Because the problem of sin is deeper than the wrong things we do and say, sin problems can only be solved by grace. Since our problem is internal, sin cannot be remedied by "getting one's act together." Only grace can bring radical heart transformation.

When the heart receives appropriate attention, children will not be able to escape how profoundly they need grace. If they see that their problem is bigger than behavior, they are delivered from superficial views of the Christian life.

Our children's needs are the same as our needs. We need the heart transplant surgery that is promised in the grace of the new covenant, "I will sprinkle clean water on you, and you will be clean; I will cleanse you from all your impurities and from all your idols" (Ezek. 36:25). Our impure thoughts and motives show how profoundly we need cleansing.

Verse 26 continues, "I will give you a new heart and put a new spirit in you; I will remove from you your heart of stone and give you a heart of flesh." What does this mean? Grace brings radical internal change. *I will remove from you your heart of stone and give you a heart of flesh.* Both our children and we need change that is radical and thorough. When a child has gained renewed interest in a toy simply because a brother would like it, that child is exhibiting a stony heart. That hardness of heart will not be melted through anything other than grace. Manipulation of behavior through rewards or punishments will never touch the stony heart. Only grace can change the heart. What encouragement! The very thing that we need is the focal point of God's work.

Not only do we need internal change, we also need empowerment. God has promised, "And I will put my Spirit in you and move you to follow my decrees and be careful to keep my laws" (Ezek. 36:27). We know what we ought to do, but we cannot do it apart from grace. We have the assurance that God's grace empowers us.

Ezekiel 36 speaks of everything we need before God: forgiveness and cleansing, radical internal change, and empowerment. The more profoundly our children know the dark caverns of the heart, the more profoundly they will understand their need for grace.

The Heart's Need for Others

When we help our children understand the subtle deceitfulness of the heart, we give them a profound alternative to independence.

the danger of being independent Independence would cut them off from the people who love them the most deeply and can be their greatest ally in the struggle against sin. Teach your children their need for your protection and direction.

Hebrews 3:12–13 is a wonderful text to demonstrate this need. "See to it, brothers, that none of you has a sinful, unbelieving heart that turns away from the living God. But encourage one another daily, as long as it is called Today, so that none of you may be hardened by sin's deceitfulness."

What is the danger? The writer warns of the danger of a sinful unbelieving heart. An unbelieving heart leads away from God.

What help is there? *But encourage one another daily.* Wise children who understand their hearts will be accessible to parents who can help them guard their hearts. Parents know them best and are the most committed to their good.

How long will we—and our children—need this kind of ministry? *As long as it is called Today*—as long as we are on this side of the heavenly kingdom.

That none of you may be hardened by sin's deceitfulness. Sin comes to deceive us, saying, "This little bitty sin is no big deal. This is a non-toxic, low-grade sin that you can enjoy without any real harm to your spiritual life." Sin deceives and hardens the heart toward God.

Sometimes bitter experience teaches our children how profoundly they need "meddlesome" parents. A friend's daughter was engaged to be married. She and her fiancée were young people who loved God and wanted to live for God's glory. One day they came to her parents confessing that they were expecting a baby. They confessed that they were given more privacy than they could handle; they had not been held accountable for long absences.

God is full of grace, mercy, and forgiveness, but these young people and their parents learned too late how profoundly they needed parental involvement.

Ministry to the Hearts of Our Children

"Brothers, if someone is caught in a sin, you who are spiritual should restore him gently. But watch yourself, or you also may be tempted" (Gal. 6:1).

Imagine that your son has behavior problems in school. You have prayed with him about his schoolday and he has promised to be good today. In the afternoon, however, you get that dreaded phone call. He has not been good. Galatians 6 gives clear insight into how to minister to your son.

Brothers, if someone is caught in a sin . . . Your son is easily entrapped. His heart, like yours, is subject to many temptations. He did not get up in the morning and say to himself, "Let's see, what could I do today that in one single act will embarrass, shame, dishonor, and frustrate my mom and dad?"

Then what happened? Why did he misbehave again? If we understand the heart, we understand the problem. Your son was entrapped because of the idols of his heart. His pride, anger, self-love, and rebellion set him up. He got caught in sin.

The Goal of Parental Intervention Is Restoration

You who are spiritual should restore him gently. You may be tempted to respond to your son's failure with anger or impatience, but your son needs restoration. Your role is to bring your child encouragement. He needs to know that there is grace, forgiveness, and mercy for those who turn to Christ.

Imagine that I had an old Victorian home in need of rehabilitation. I could demolish the home and build a new one in its place, or I could restore the old one. If my choice was restoration, I would use a different set of tools than I would use for demolition. Parents, particularly of teens, often come to their children with the wrecking-ball approach. They blister their ears with angry and destructive words. They may desire to restore, but after the wrecking ball has finished with a house, there is little left to restore.

If the goal is restoration, what tools will we take to the job? We will take our knowledge of the Scripture, along with deep insight into the treachery of the human heart, compassionate understanding, and great hope in the power and grace of the gospel. We will speak the truth in love to this child who has become entrapped by his sin. We will shine the light of God's truth on the messy situation. We want this child to know that there is a powerful God who can rescue people who have become entrapped.

RESTORATION REQUIRES A GENTLE TOUCH

You who are spiritual should restore him gently. One winter's day in the midst of a snowstorm I had a car accident. What could have been life-threatening instead resulted in some bad bruises and abrasions due to God's mercy, through the means of airbags and good engineering. The EMTs were gentle and kind. They did not blame me for making them venture out into the storm or throw me roughly into the back of the ambulance. Why were they so gentle? Their object was my restoration. Gentleness will facilitate restoration for our children.

Restoration Requires Humility

Galatians 6 also calls us to humility. While the word humble is not used in the passage, the concept is present. *But watch yourself, or you also may be tempted.* What temptations have our children fallen into that we never experience? Have they been unkind, spoken out of turn, reacted in anger, responded in pride, or been deceitful? Do we sometimes fall prey to these sins? Restoration is a wonderful time to stand in solidarity with our children as parents who can humbly identify with their failures and point them to the willing, able, and powerful Savior of sinners.

Solomon prayed at the dedication of the Temple, "May the LORD our God be with us as he was with our fathers; may he never leave us or forsake us. May he turn our hearts to him, to walk in all his ways and to keep the commands, decrees and regulations he gave our fathers" (1 Kings 8:57–58).

CHAPTER 6

The Sowing and Reaping Principle of Scripture

Scripture bursts with teaching about God's design for consequences as a demonstration of his sovereignty over all things and as a sanctifying process for his people. Illustrations of sowing and reaping fill the narratives and prophecies of biblical history. The epistles also teem with exhortations and examples of sowing and reaping.

Probably the most familiar passage to all of us is Galatians 6:7–8. "Do not be deceived: God cannot be mocked. A man reaps what he sows. The one who sows to please his sinful nature, from that nature will reap destruction; the one who sows to please the Spirit, from the Spirit will reap eternal life."

Our central objective in instruction, discipline and correction is heart change, not behavior change. This profoundly shapes how we view consequences. Consequences are not disconnected from the shepherding process—they are a vital part! But children must understand consequences as God designed them, not as the world teaches them!

Our goal in discipline is to reach the heart of our child. We don't want to use consequences only to shape behavior. Behaviorism (behavior modification) is constraining and controlling behavior through a system of rewards and punishments, sometimes called "the carrot and the stick." Behavioristic consequences may be authoritarian (Gestapo-like) and threatening, or simply manipulative, promising

goal: heart change

material or emotional reward. They may offer external incentives and disincentives to change behavior, or they may appeal to a child's sense of guilt and fear of disapproval. These methods are powerful tools to change behavior, but they abandon the child's heart!

In contrast, biblical correction, discipline and motivation use the enduring truth of Scripture to instruct the heart and direct behavior. Since God is concerned with our hearts as the source of our behavior, it follows that heart change is our most important concern as we instruct and discipline our children, encouraging them to live consistently with God's law.

Christian parents can confuse God's role and their role in parenting. We have God's standard—his law, which we hold out for our children. Since we cannot reach into their hearts and change them, the temptation is to substitute the behavioristic methods of the culture for the power of the Word of God and the work of his Spirit in the hearts of our children. The culture depends on behaviorism because they do not have any doctrine of internal change.

You might ask then, "What role do consequences have in this process? Can I shepherd my child's heart and still have consequences for behavior? Will that confuse them? If the heart is the battleground, then why would I correct external behavior?" The sowing and reaping principle described and illustrated in Scripture helps us understand and practice God's plan for consequences in the discipline process. You must understand this process yourself. You must self-consciously teach it to your children. They must see God's discipline and your correction as a blessing and protection to keep them from foolishness and destruction.

Without this vision for heart change, your instruction, correction, motivation and consequences will become a desperate attempt to get your children in line. You will be satisfied with external change in behavior rather than training the hearts of your children.

We have the hope of the heart- and life-transforming power of the gospel. The gospel is your only hope for true change of heart in your children. All of your instruction and consequences must be energized by this truth. God has ordained that, "The unfolding of your words gives light" (Ps. 119:130). Your parenting task is to bring truth. God changes hearts. Behavior follows the heart. Even when you must constrain behavior, you must have a bigger objective in view—to bring God's truth to your children. Since God's Word addresses the child's heart, you must also be focused on the heart.

Help your children understand the distinction between behavioristic consequences and biblical sowing and reaping. There are two reasons why this is important. First, we must understand, and teach our children to understand, the errors of popular culture as it imposes itself on our philosophy of life and practice. Secondly, if your child is to benefit fully in God's redemptive purposes in chastisement—he must own it as a precious act of reclamation and preservation by God—not as a random or capricious cosmic zap from the Almighty. You stand as God's agent of loving standard-bearing and caring instruction. You administer temporal and tactile reminders—consequences—to instill the truth that God cannot be mocked.

Sowing and Reaping

The sowing and reaping principle of Scripture provides a paradigm for understanding biblical consequences. The most dramatic difference between biblical consequences and behaviorist consequences is the goal of consequences. As parents apply the sowing and reaping principle of Scripture, the consequences they shape will serve as a small part of the discipline process, to underscore the reality of biblical truth. In contrast, because behavioristic consequences serve solely as a means to change behavior, they direct children away from the gospel and lasting heart change.

heart change vs beh. change

A Biblical Vision for Sowing and Reaping

I recently heard the phrase, "We reap what we sow!" in a car advertisement. While popular culture regards the concept loosely as getting what you deserve, it falls far short of both the temporal and eternal consequences for behavior described in Scripture. What is sowing and reaping? And how can you redeem God's holy purpose for this process in the shepherding of your children? How should you think about this "sowing and reaping" equation?

THE BLESSINGS OF SOWING TO THE SPIRIT

Galatians 6:8 encourages us, "He who sows to the Spirit reaps eternal life." Use the illustrations, commands, callings and promises of Scripture and church history to embolden and ennoble children's minds and hearts to pursue holiness and put sin to death. Be careful to represent the blessings of life in the Spirit as beautiful and life-giving, even when you must point out the folly and disaster of disobedience and law-breaking.

Another way the Bible presents the sowing metaphor is with the language of planting and harvest. If we plant peas, we will harvest peas. We can't sow seeds of sinful thoughts and behavior and reap anything other than what we've sown. Sometimes our children sow sin and pray for crop failure! It won't happen. God has so ordained life that there are outcomes that are inevitable. You must learn to live and train your children to live with a "harvest mindset." They are always sowing and always reaping. This process happens scores of times each day. What children plant today will be harvested tomorrow. "Tomorrow" may be measured by moments or years, but it will come.

Sowing and Reaping Is a Biblical Reality

The sowing and reaping principle of Scripture is a statement of fact! It is based on God's covenant. Remember that there were blessings and curses attached to God's covenant with man; first with Adam, then with the patriarchs, followed by his chosen people, Israel (illustrated in Deuteronomy 28), and extended in the new covenant to all believers. The sowing and reaping principle of Scripture reflects the outcomes or consequences that God has built into his world. God's consequences are undeniable. They are sovereign and holy. They are deeply spiritual, supernatural and eternal as well as temporal. Sowing to the sinful nature brings destruction, both in time and eternity. Sowing to the Spirit brings peace with God and the spiritual comfort of his nearness, even in the midst of fallen and painful life experience, and results in eternal life. As we look at life in this world, we find that this truth of Scripture is demonstrated and authenticated to us over and over again in personal relationships, in circumstances, in the physical universe and in corporate life.

1 Samuel 2:30 provides a case study in biblical sowing and reaping:

> Therefore the LORD, the God of Israel, declares: 'I promised that your house and your father's house would minister before me forever.' But now the LORD declares: 'Far be it from me! Those who honor me I will honor, but those who despise me will be disdained.'

Eli was a priest in God's house. He knew the blessings and curses of God's covenant with Israel. His failure to curb his son's desires and the ensuing death of his family, the loss of the priesthood for future generations for his family and his grief and sorrow of heart were not just a threat that God held over his head. These awful pronouncements were the inevitable consequences of Eli's choice to sow disobedience to God as he raised his sons. He earned in his life and spirit the full sentence of his choices.

BEHAVIORISTIC CONSEQUENCES OF SOWING AND REAPING FROM SCRIPTURE

Our culture sees sowing and reaping as Santa-like. "You better watch out. You better not cry. You better not pout, I'm tellin' you why." The majority culture acknowledges only the material world. They have left God's sovereign superintendence of his universe out of the picture. So, consequences have only to do with the lusts and desires of life. Therefore, as an ad gimmick to justify my lust for an automobile, this concept seems perfectly logical.

Parents, as tangible representatives of God's authority, must <u>understand and practice biblical consequences *rather than* the rewards and punishments of behaviorism.</u> The sowing and reaping principle shows the way. *[handwritten margin note: biblical consequence vs behavior]*

First, we will expose the deception. How is behaviorism different from sowing and reaping?

Rewards / Punishments of Behaviorism	Biblical Sowing and Reaping Principles
1. Goal: Consequences are an external attempt to change behavior—what will appeal to the child enough to be a motivator or sting enough to be a deterrent. Without an ethical or moral foundation, we have a changing standard. Children grow bitter and feel justified in rebellion. Behavioristic rewards develop a sense of rights (I deserve . . .) in a child. Random punishments that reflect the caprice and mood of the parent cause the root of bitterness and rebellion to grow and flourish.	1. Goal: Consequences only serve to underscore the principles and absolutes of Scripture with temporal outcomes. The fixed foundation of God's truth is the basis for morality and ethics. "Thus saith the Lord" is sufficient reason for avoiding sin and striving for good.
	Consequences are rooted in the principles and absolutes of Scripture and the provision of saving and sanctifying grace to reflect the covenant God has established with man for either blessing or cursing. Training appeals to a higher standard that children can anticipate because it is outside human fickleness—outside our preference or the whim of the moment.
	Consequences enable our joyful obedience to our Savior. The gospel shines with hope in the face of our sin and inability.
	There is hope!

Rewards / Punishments of Behaviorism	Biblical Sowing and Reaping Principles
2. Consequences are generally unrelated to behavior. Popular behavioristic tactics such as time out, grounding and loss of stuff do not bear out biblical truth all by themselves. They simply serve as power plays to prove our power of persuasion through deprivation of their stuff and privileges. This plants seeds of rebellion in a child's already defiant heart.	2. Consequences should be related as closely as possible to the occasion of discipline. Irresponsibility should result in loss of privilege or restitution for sin. Our goal in the choice of consequence is to display the reality of life in God's world. God has created and he sustains all things by the Word of his power. He has established law that brings glory to himself and safety and protection to his creatures. Refusal to live in his ways in his world results in disaster both in time and eternity.

There is precedent for this truth everywhere in the Scriptures. "All who draw the sword will die by the sword" (Matt. 26:52). "If a king judges the poor with fairness, his throne will always be secure" (Prov. 29:14).

Remember Miriam in Numbers 12? In her pride, she demanded recognition in the assembly of the Israelites as Moses and Aaron's sister. She was discontent with her humble place. What did she reap? Leprosy! She was cast out of the assembly and suffered loneliness and disgrace because of her sin of pride and her demand to be lifted up.

In Numbers 20:1–13, Moses became angry with the complaining, quarrelsome, unbelieving Israelites. He struck the rock in anger rather than entrusting himself to God and bringing godly direction to his people. God said, "Because you did not trust in me enough to honor me as holy in the sight of the Israelites, you will not bring this community into the land I give them." What was the goal of this sojourn in the desert? The goal was to enter the Promised Land.

3. Consequences are event oriented and temporary. They are focused on changing behavior, getting the problem solved so that life can go on uninterrupted.	3. Consequences are process oriented. They are honestly goal directed for the child's eternal benefit so that future temptations will be a reminder of godly lessons learned in previous heart skirmishes.
4. Consequences are concerned with controlling and constraining behavior for wrong motives—for looks, convenience and pride.	4. Consequences are concerned with fruit that endures and builds character and godly values for use in God's kingdom. God disciplines his people to produce holiness in them.

Overwhelmingly, God's purpose in chastisement is to promote righteousness. Hebrews 12:5–7 and 10–12 show us God's heart toward his people:

> And you have forgotten that word of encouragement that addresses you as sons: "My son, do not make light of the Lord's discipline, and do not lose heart when he rebukes you, because the Lord disciplines those he loves, and he punishes everyone he accepts as a son." Endure hardship as discipline; God is treating you as sons. For what son is not disciplined by his father?
>
> Our fathers disciplined us for a little while as they thought best; but God disciplines us for our good, that we may share in his holiness. No discipline seems pleasant at the time, but painful. Later on, however, it produces a harvest of righteousness and peace for those who have been trained by it. Therefore, strengthen your feeble arms and weak knees.

What a radical worldview! Reaping, in God's purposes for his people, is to restore. Is that how children think of reaping at your hand, even when they must suffer painful consequences for their sin?

5. Consequences reflect the authorities' personal standards and goals.	5. Consequences reflect the Law of God as the standard for morality and ethics, and the path of blessing, peace, hope and restoration.

Consequences that reflect God's law will be consistent and will emphasize the long-term good of our children. Let me illustrate. One day I may prefer that my children put coats on before going into the chilly fall temperatures. I may give humanistic reasons for my requirement of them. "I am worried about your health. You'll catch pneumonia out there without protection." "You have to obey me, and I think it's too cold to go out without a coat! Remember your father said you were to obey me today or you would 'get it' when he gets home tonight!"

You may threaten punishment for not obeying and respond in anger if they do not comply. The very next day, you may have other more pressing issues on your mind, and you may not even care whether they go out without coat and hat in even more inclement weather than the previous day. You may say, "I don't care. Just give me some peace and quiet. If you catch cold, it's your own dumb fault!"

In a biblical vision, my standards must be supported by the principles and absolutes of Scripture to have moral and ethical clout when I bring them to my children, mixed and served up with the grace and compassion of the gospel. It may sound like this. "I want you to put warm clothes on and your hat and coat before you go out to play. I know you feel like it's still warm enough to play without wraps, but my judgment is that you need them. Trust me. I love you and will never knowingly ask you to do anything that will injure you. Remember that a wise man heeds instruction. And a wise child brings joy to his mother's heart. God promises spiritual blessing to the child who overcomes personal preferences to heed the instruction of parents. If you are tempted to disobey, remember that I am always ready to pray with you for God's promised help in your temptation. I love you and I know how hard it is to do what your authority asks rather than what your own will directs you to do. God will give you strength to choose wisdom rather than foolishness."

This is important formative instruction. We need to think clearly and train our children to understand consequences in light of biblical sowing and reaping. They need instruction that exposes them to who God is and what he has done, and what his purposes are for his people. They must understand the sowing and reaping principles of the Scripture as a basis for the consequences they harvest—both positive consequences and negative consequences.

Two Types of Consequences

There are two types of consequences: natural consequences and consequences shaped by authorities.

Natural consequences are those that happen if no one interferes. When I get angry and kick something, my toe hurts. In the same way, a child's failure to pack his school lunch should result in a growling stomach, not a McDonald's Happy Meal. Losing the calculator, again, should result in doing math the old fashioned way, not another trip to the mall for an even "cooler" calculator. Parents often shield their children from the very natural consequences for behavior that would serve to get the child's attention to change in obvious areas of irresponsible behavior.

Consequences shaped by authority are those where the authority determines the outcome that is called for *to underscore the principle or absolute in Scripture.* Notice my definition—authorities do not have the right to shape consequences so that children learn "to never do that again if they know what's good for them," or "to show them I'm not stupid," or "they can't get away with that stuff with me!" Consequences are not intended to establish my standards or rights or intelligence (although that will be a by-product of the authentic goal). Help children to recognize that consequences are not "what I am doing to you," but "what you have brought about by the choices you have made." "*You* are reaping what *you* have sown!" Children who gripe to their friends, "You won't believe what my mother is doing to me now!" don't understand. They are harvesting their own crop, not Mom's. This consequence is the result of their own choices—even if their mother has designed the results. When the goal is short-term behavioral change rather than long-term character development, children consider parents their adversaries rather than facilitators of godly character growth.

Biblical consequences must be *reasonable* and *logical*. They cannot be extreme or excessive. God's ways protect us from overdoing consequences out of anger, frustration, fear or a perceived need to control our children or family circumstances. If we are focused on teaching our children's hearts, we are not likely to give in to the motivators for behaviorism that we contrasted earlier.

Consequences must be logical—connected as closely as possible to what has gone wrong. Consequences should truly serve the goals of discipline and correction—to disciple. To disciple our children, we must understand and instruct our children that there are spiritual dimensions of sowing and reaping.

Spiritual Dimensions of Sowing and Reaping

Reaping is always more than the immediate temporal consequence. We do not want to depend on consequences to alter the child's behavior. The reaping process has spiritual dimensions that the world does not consider or acknowledge.

God uniquely designed man to respond to spiritual and unseen reality. We are always explaining, interpreting, defining and interacting with the sensory world with our spiritual being.

Galatians 6:7–8 reminds us of the spiritual and eternal dimensions of sowing and reaping. Sowing to the sinful nature, or flesh, brings destruction. Sowing to the Spirit brings eternal life. We become focused on temporal, immediate rewards and forget God's reminders that life is more than what we wear, what we eat, and what we can see and touch and feel. There is always an unseen world of spiritual reality when God trains us.

What are some of the reaping considerations that we must teach our children if we understand this spiritual dimension of sowing and reaping? The most significant consequences are not always immediate or readily identifiable. The consequences we shape serve to highlight these inevitable outcomes.

Suppose Johnny fails to do his chores through disobedience or laziness. What are the issues we need to discuss with Johnny? What inevitable spiritual consequences accompany Johnny's choices even before I address his disobedience? What should the tangible consequences he receives serve to teach him?

There are at least these six inevitable consequences of all thoughts and actions before any consequences are handed out by temporal authorities.

We Reap in Relationship with God

God will not be mocked. "For a man's ways are in full view of the LORD, and he examines all his paths" (Prov. 5:21). God is our friend or enemy (Jas. 4:4). God thwarts the conniving of the double-minded (Jas. 1:6–8). We are either hot or cold spiritually (Rev. 3:15–16). Lukewarm is for plumbing; it is not a spiritual option. We gather or scatter because of our thoughts and deeds (Matt. 12:30). We will either live with a sense of biblical well-being or guilt and fear. Remember the blessings and curses of the covenant. Either we will be God's holy people or he will disown us.

> See to it, brothers, that none of you has a sinful, unbelieving heart that turns away from the living God. But encourage one another daily, as long as it is called Today, so that none of you may be hardened by sin's deceitfulness.
>
> —Hebrews 3:12–13

We can be hardened by the deceitfulness of sin, which separates us from communion with God. Calluses on our hands aid us when we grasp hot beverages, but calluses on the heart are devastating. When we sin, and repentance is not our first response, we reap in relationship to God. God seems distant and out of reach. Spiritual reality seems illusive and ephemeral. Johnny is reaping. His disobedience hardens his heart to God.

There are two ways this truth works out. For the unbeliever, his temporal and eternal life is always at stake. Apart from repentance and faith, we are always storing up for ourselves wrath against the Day of Judgment (Rom. 2:5). The unbeliever is separated from God and doomed to eternal destruction. The gospel is the only hope for him to be restored to relationship with God and escape from eternal death because of Christ's work. What a consequence! What an opportunity to bring the grace and mercy of God into the discipline and correction of our children! They are reaping every day in relationship to God. This does not *become* a reality because they believe in God. It *is* the reality in which we all live! [it already is reality]

For the believer, who has repented and believed in the Lord Jesus Christ, his justification is sure. He is not in danger of eternal destruction. However, we have constant warnings in Scripture of two dangers. First, if we are not truly repentant, we will be like the seed that seemed to grow for a time, but then was choked by the cares of life (Mk. 4:1–20). It is possible to assent to the truth in theory, but not in practice. Secondly, we can develop coldness of heart toward God. "Drawing near" to God encourages growth in grace (Heb. 10:19–25), but a straying heart cannot maintain daily communion and fellowship with God.

In contrast, sowing devotion and longing for God and his kingdom brings spiritual blessings that are expressed in rapturous language throughout the Scriptures. Psalm 37:4 captures the harvest of the soul, "Delight yourself in the LORD and he will give you the desires of your heart." We reap in relationship to God!

We Reap in Habits for Life

Habits of thought and practice in childhood will prove immovable in adult life. Daily choices that may seem insignificant as a single event, gather momentum that results in shaping our character. It is inevitable. The heart that conceives deceitful ways of living solves life's daily challenges by lying, cheating, thievery and treachery. The heart that conceives honest ways of living solves life's daily challenges by truth-telling, integrity, respect for the person and property of others, and honoring and obeying proper authorities. All the single choices "clump together" to become the most comfortable response to the people and circumstances of everyday life. We all would acknowledge that habits of life are formed in early youth, and if left unchallenged by outside influences set the course for life. We reap in habits for life.

Johnny has tailor-made opportunities in his family chores to practice and demonstrate habits of healthy community living. His neglect of these duties will reinforce patterns of irresponsibility in other areas of family and school life and eventually, life in the workplace.

What will this look like in ten years? Children who throw temper fits when they can't have their brother's toy "right now" when they are three years old, will storm out of the house in rebellion when you don't give permission for their wants when they are fourteen years old. The child who hides the broken vase when he is four years old, rather than telling you that he broke it, will forge your name on school correspondence to hide a bad report or lie to save face when confronted with his sin as a teen. We reap in habits for life.

In contrast, when God circumcises the heart, he provides the Spirit to motivate us to follow his decrees and to be careful to keep his laws (Ezek. 36:25–27). What a glorious incentive for parents to encourage their children to consider reaping in habits for life. It is the context in which we may remind them of God's ability and willingness to change their hearts and habits as they confess their need. We reap in habits for life!

We Reap in Reputation

Our reputation is the sum of impressions others have of us. It is defined by the ways we respond to others and to the circumstances of life. Children want to be regarded as good, reliable, dependable, trustworthy, honest, kind and so forth. Children don't recognize that an inevitable consequence of their attitudes and behavior is their reputation. "How I hated discipline! How my heart spurned correction! I would not obey my teachers or listen to my instructors. I have come to the brink of utter ruin in the midst of the whole assembly" (Prov. 5:12–14).

Johnny has a reputation regarding trash removal. In fact, when Mom asks his sister Sally to do the dishes, Sally says, "I don't know why I have to do the dishes! Johnny never takes the trash out!"

Matthew 5:13–16, the familiar salt and light passage, is about reputation. Its content and purpose are clear. Reputation serves as a preservative from corruption and as a light shining in the dark world for the purpose of bringing praise to God. Children need to learn to ask themselves, "What effect will my attitude and behavior have on the people in my world. <u>How will this affect my opportunities, privileges, and usefulness in the kingdom of God?</u>"

Children should be reminded that authorities in our youth may turn out to be our colleagues of the future, or our students, or our parishioners, or even our in-laws! We now have a son-in-law and daughter-in-law who were students in our Sunday school and Christian school classrooms as children. They are now co-workers in Christ's kingdom and neighbors as adults! We reap in reputation!

We Reap in Human Relationships

Our behavior has great implications for our relationships with family, peers and authorities. Johnny and his parents have a breakdown in relationship every week that Johnny does not care for his responsibility to take out the trash. It even carries over to other areas of their relationship.

Our relationships will be open and free or filled with fear, guilt, hurt, bitterness, regret and defensiveness. Children frequently exhibit attitudes and behaviors as if these choices had no influence on relationships. They want relationships to go on unaltered by sinful attitudes and behavior. Unfortunately, even many adults have never learned this lesson. We reap enormous beauty or pain in relationships, depending on what we sow! Relationships are either facilitated or stopped dead by the attitudes and choices of the individuals in a relationship. The ordinary conflicts of life that fill our days with potential offenses do not call for rebuffs—rather for Christ-like remediation. We reap in relationships!

We Reap in Long-Term Usefulness in Christ's Kingdom

We are all players in God's amazing redemptive pageant. The story is about his glory and his law and his grace displayed in Christ Jesus, with its final scene before the throne of God in the new heavens and the new earth! Life, for believers, consists in sowing heart attitudes and behaviors that facilitate these grand themes of God's pageant, that rehearse the beauty and symmetry of his law, that practice its precepts and bask in the spiritual blessings of living in the light. Heart attitudes and behaviors that sow conflict with this message leave the believer ineffective and unproductive.

Let me illustrate. In the small Christian junior high school where I was principal, some of the girls were having trouble getting along. As I looked into the teacher's report, I learned that one of the girls was gossiping and stirring up dissension within the group. What was ironic was that this same girl requested prayer often that she would be a Christian witness amongst her friends. She genuinely desired to minister the gospel in her relationships—but she neglected to consider the implications of her speech and behavior for her usefulness in Christ's kingdom.

Consider the story of the prodigal son. He was received back into the family. Relationship was restored, but the inheritance and its usefulness for good was lost, respect for his station was diminished, wasted years meant lost opportunities. We reap in long-term usefulness in Christ's kingdom!

We Reap for Eternity

Unbelievers who suppress the truth in ungodliness will reap a harvest. This is not only the warning of Scripture to flee the wrath to come, it is a statement of the reality in which we live. Unbelievers, blinded by the deceiver to believe that all is well, to live for the moment, are piling up the outcomes we have already described. They are also storing up wrath for the Day of Judgment.

"The wicked man earns deceptive wages [he may even get away with it now], but he who sows righteousness reaps a sure reward" [eternity tells the real story] (Prov. 11:18).

Believers reap for eternity too. Certainly, all who have repented and believed will enjoy the new heavens and the new earth. They will see the Savior face to face. But we have indications in the Scriptures that our sowing in this present life will have implications for the crowns we will lay at his feet. There appear to be degrees of glorying in his presence. Just as surely as our longing for Christ's kingdom has implications for our everyday experience of fellowship with the Spirit and the comfort of his presence, so the sum of our life of sowing to the Spirit has implications for our eternal enjoyment of Glory. "If any man builds on this foundation using gold, silver, costly stones, wood, hay or straw, his work will be shown for what it is, because the Day will bring it to light. It will be revealed with fire, and the fire will test the quality of each man's work. If what he has built survives, he will receive his reward. If it is burned up, he will suffer loss; he himself will be saved, but only as one escaping through the flames" (1 Cor. 3:12–15). Lest we think of heaven as the great "fire escape" and seek to attain it by "the skin of our teeth," we should consider the beauty of living for Christ alone—not for fire insurance—but for sheer wonder at his stooping to own us and preparing mansions for us and delighting in us!

Teaching It to Our Children

Let's be honest. We think of consequences or reaping, as negative—something God does *to* us rather than *for* us. And we tend to use these truths about God to beat up our children spiritually in a desperate attempt to keep them on the straight and narrow. The truth is that sowing and reaping are wonderful mercies of God to inhibit sinful desires and show the paths of life. Consequences should be presented in that light.

Take the time to tell your children the truth about sowing and reaping. Use this chapter as an outline for your instruction. Illustrate and practice biblical sowing and reaping in your home. Keep a family notebook of illustrations of sowing and reaping that you find in the Scriptures, in church history, and in family and community life. You will find a lot in the news. Identify and rejoice over positive illustrations, laugh at the comic illustrations in everyday life, comfort one another and pray over the sad and painful illustrations, seek God to learn from them and to find the courage and faith to sow to the Spirit rather than to the flesh. Consequences are deterrents and protection against sowing to the flesh.

Behavioristic rewards and punishments don't teach these powerful spiritual lessons. Consequences that manipulate behavior and do not train the heart are merely external props that will result in moral and ethical collapse and eternity without God.

Understand and practice the sowing and reaping principle of Scripture in your life. Teach it to your children. It will automatically transform the way you practice correction and discipline in your home.

Implications

Behaviorism may be popular—it may even work, but it obscures the gospel. When we can use incentives or punishments to get the behavior we want without God and his redemption, we are teaching our children that they can live in God's world without Christ and do just fine, thank you!

How can we honestly bring consequences to our children that mirror the sowing and reaping principles of Scripture?

We must be students of the Scriptures. We cannot understand God's truth without reading and studying his Word. Moses disclosed the importance of God's revelation when he addressed the Israelites after restating the Law before his death. In Deuteronomy 32:45–47 we read, "When Moses finished reciting all these words to all Israel, he said to them, 'Take to heart all the words I have solemnly declared to you this day, so that you may command your children to obey carefully all the words of this law. They are not just idle words for you—they are your life. By them you will live long in the land you are crossing the Jordan to possess.'"

Prayer is an essential element of biblical understanding and use of consequences in the discipline process. Pray over the consequences that you shape to underscore the truth of Scripture. Don't talk to your children about that which you have spoken little with God.

Self-shepherding is the best preparation for practical application of consequences for your children. Deuteronomy 6:6 reminds us, "These commandments that I give you today are to be upon *your* hearts." Then verse 7 says, "Impress them on your children."

James 3:13–18 provides a contrast that will help children understand sowing and reaping. "Who is wise and understanding among you? Let him show it by his good life, by deeds done in the humility that comes from wisdom. But if you harbor bitter envy and selfish ambition in your hearts, do not boast about it or deny the truth. Such 'wisdom' does not come down from heaven but is earthly, unspiritual, of the devil. For where you have envy and selfish ambition, there you find disorder and every evil practice. But the wisdom that comes from heaven is first of all pure; then peace-loving, considerate, submissive, full of mercy and good fruit, impartial and sincere. Peacemakers who sow in peace raise a harvest of righteousness."

CHAPTER 7

Authority Is God's Plan

What do you think of when you hear the word "authority"? We limit our ideas of authority to either overwhelming force (someone rules because they have power that cannot be resisted) or ruling by consent (someone rules because the people have given their permission). The Bible teaches that it is good and proper for some people to be *in* authority and for other people to be *under* authority.

God has structured the world he made with a particular order. There is a plan to the relationships his creatures have with himself and with each other. Those relationships could be called horizontal and vertical. For example, we live in the modern world, where there is an emphasis on the inherent equality of people. If we drew a picture of that concept, people would be horizontal to each other. But when we reflect on the fact that there is hierarchy in creation, or caregivers and care-receivers, a vertical picture unfolds. Just as there are "vertical" relationships *between* God and human beings, angels and human beings, and human beings and the creatures, so also there are vertical relationships *among* human beings. The following section will discuss hierarchy in creation, and how that extends to specific vertical relationships among people, focusing on the relationship between parents and children.

Hierarchy in Creation

God's Relationship with Humankind

Psalm 8 describes the majesty and glory of God. "O LORD, our Lord, how majestic is your name in all the earth! You have set your glory above the heavens." God is over all. God's relationship to people is vertical. The Psalm extols the wonders of the creation and marvels that God would still be interested in humanity. "When I consider your heavens, the work of your fingers, the moon and the stars, which you have set in place, what is man that you are mindful of him, the son of man that you care for him?" (Ps. 8:3–4).

Humankind's place is under God, the Creator, who cares for his creation. "He causes his sun to rise on the evil and the good, and sends rain on the righteous and the unrighteous" (Matt. 5:45; see also Acts 14:17; 1 Pet. 5:7).

The Angels' Relationship with Humankind

People are also under a whole category of heavenly creatures, the angels, who are always in the presence of God. Even though people are not the highest of all created beings, they are still creatures of great dignity. "You made him a little lower than the heavenly beings and crowned him with glory and honor" (Ps. 8:5).

The angels are God's messengers to care for his people. "For he will command his angels concerning you to guard you in all your ways; they will lift you up in their hands, so that you will not strike your foot against a stone" (Ps. 91:11–12; see also Matt. 18:10 and Lk. 16:22).

Humankind's Relationship to the Earthly Creation

"You made him ruler over the works of your hands; you put everything under his feet: all flocks and herds, and the beasts of the field, the birds of the air, and the fish of the sea, all that swim the paths of the seas" (Ps. 8:6–8). The Bible requires those in authority to care for, provide for, and protect those under their authority. God is the model for the one in authority. He loves, provides, protects, and defends. People are the designated caretakers of creation. Their rule over the animals and the rest of creation should imitate God's care, and should never result in cruelty, carelessness, or destruction.

In summary, there is hierarchy in the created order. God created and assigned to each part of his creation its place in the universe.

- Man, male and female, is made in the image of God (Gen. 1:27).
- God has given him dominion over all the creation (Gen. 1:28).
- God has put all things under his feet (Ps. 8:6).

- Man has both the right and the responsibility to rule and exercise the authority God has given him in the creation (Gen. 1:26, 28).
- Man is a steward of all that God has created. He is higher than all other created beings on earth (Ps. 8:5–6).
- He has the responsibility to rule the beasts, birds, and sea creatures (Ps. 8:6–8).

Hierarchy in People's Relationships to Each Other

We cannot teach our children how to submit to an authority unless we understand a vertical structure where equals willingly place themselves under authority.

It is true that human relationships are horizontal in terms of worth and dignity. All human beings are made in God's image, are crowned with glory and honor, and are given rule over the rest of creation. In relationship to God and saving grace all human beings are equal; all come to God on the same basis and God is no respecter of persons. But at the same time, God has established spheres of authority and responsibility for mankind.

The contemporary mind has only two ways to respond to authority— rebellion or servility. We do not understand the idea of being an intelligent, independent, thinking person who is willing to be under authority. *authority is not bad* We need to learn that submission is dignified and noble. It is not servile and foolish. The Bible requires those *under* authority to respect and submit to leadership. Submission is enjoying the strength and honor of serving one's Lord by serving the authority he put in place.

God has placed people in authority in the workplace, in the church, in the state, and in the home. Lording it over those under our authority, making others servile, is a wicked perversion and a defacing of God's image.

Authority in the Workplace

Those who are in authority are responsible to care for those who work for them. "Masters, provide your slaves with what is right and fair, because you know that you also have a Master in heaven" (Col. 4:1). "You shall not defraud your neighbor or rob him. Do not hold back the wages of a hired man overnight" (Lev. 19:13).

Those who are under authority are responsible to be cooperative with their bosses. "Slaves, obey your earthly masters in everything;

and do it, not only when their eye is on you and to win their favor, but with sincerity of heart and reverence for the Lord" (Col. 3:22; see also Eph. 6:5 and Tit. 2:9).

Submission to authority does not signify inferiority, only difference in role and sphere of responsibility. There is an interesting passage in 1 Timothy 6 that reconciles submission and equality. "All who are under the yoke of slavery should consider their masters worthy of full respect, so that God's name and our teaching may not be slandered. Those who have believing masters are not to show less respect for them because they are brothers. Instead, they are to serve them even better, because those who benefit from their service are believers, and dear to them. These are the things you are to teach and urge on them" (1 Tim. 6:1–2).

Authority in the Church

God has established authority structures in the church. Elders, pastors, or overseers, are called to direct the affairs of the church (1 Tim. 5:17). "Be shepherds of God's flock that is under your care, serving as overseers—not because you must, but because you are willing, as God wants you to be; not greedy for money, but eager to serve; not lording it over those entrusted to you, but being examples to the flock" (1 Pet. 5:2–3).

People under their care are to listen to them and heed what they say (Heb. 13:17).

Authority in the State

God has established authority structures in the state. The civil authority is God's servant and exercises authority that God has given (Rom. 13:1–4). The civil authority makes laws, defends its citizens, charges taxes (Matt. 22:17–21), and punishes evildoers (1 Pet. 2:14).

It is written in 1 Peter 2:13–14 "Submit yourselves for the Lord's sake to every authority instituted among men: whether to the king, as the supreme authority, or to governors, who are sent by him to punish those who do wrong and to commend those who do right" (see also 1 Tim. 2:1–2; Tit. 3:1).

Authority in the Home

God has established authority structures in the home. Men are to provide loving leadership, laying down their lives for their wives

(Eph. 5:25–33). Wives are to receive and follow the leadership of their husbands (Eph. 5:22–24). Children are to honor and obey their parents (Eph. 6:1–3).

Hierarchy in Parent and Child Relationships

It is sweet and seemly for parents to rule and for children to submit. Instructing our children regarding the authority structures that God has created will form their thinking about the very concept of authority. This formative instruction is far more profound than merely training our children to obey. It gives them a model of how God has made things and how they are all supposed to function.

Our society is confused about authority. Arrogant children give orders to their parents. Parents lament but cannot control the hours their children spend on TV and video games. Biblical concepts of authority and responsibility have been replaced with negotiation and compromise.

When our children clearly understand that authority structures come from God, obedience to parents will not seem to be a random requirement. It will be clear that obedience is an opportunity to be part of the order and beauty of creation and is an act of trust in God.

Circle of Blessing

God has drawn a circle in Ephesians 6:1–3 in which children are to live. The boundaries of the circle are honor and obedience. Children are to submit to the authority of their parents.

The majority culture thinks of authority as despotism and submission as servile. Many parents question the fairness of being authorities. They reason, since I do not like it when someone tells me to submit to authority, my children will not like it either. So parents give away their authority. Children are allowed to choose what they will wear, what activities they will engage in, what they will eat, and who they will spend time with. By the age that they are ready for school, most children see themselves as autonomous decision-makers. Parents give away their authority in thousands of transactions.

"Honey, I am sorry. I forgot that you don't like oatmeal. Let's see, would you like some Sugar Smacks or Cocoa Puffs?"

How much better it would be for a parent to kindly say, "Honey, I know that oatmeal is not your favorite. Maybe another day we will have something you enjoy more, but it is good, nutritious food. We are going to pray, thanking God for it, and eat it with a cheerful heart."

There is a popular method of child management that powerfully illustrates my point. "Honey, you can wear the red shirt, the green shirt, or the blue shirt. It's up to you."

It does not occur to a three-year-old that there are more than three shirts in the closet. He makes his choice. Mother is indifferent to which shirt the child chooses. All are equally appropriate. On the surface it seems like a win, win. The child feels like he is a decision-maker, mother gets him to wear something appropriate, and there is no fight. What could be better than that?

does it really harm my child to let them choose their clothes?

While all that sounds very good and quite enlightened, in reality the subtext for the child is, "You are the decision-maker here. You have the right to choose. I may suggest the various alternatives, but it is your right to choose."

We as a culture are not shocked by this scheme and it doesn't even seem inappropriate because we see the world as fundamentally horizontal. This child is not learning that God, who is good, has given him parents whom he is to obey; and it is a blessing to live under God's authority. He is rather being taught to reject any authority other than himself.

When we make our children independent decision-makers, we give them an appetite for a liberty that does not exist and a mistaken notion about freedom. This liberty does not exist because individual freedom with no authorities does not exist in the will of God for creatures. We are always people under authority. Freedom *is not* being able to do whatever you want; freedom *is* knowing and loving God and living joyfully under the authority structures that he has ordained. "I will always obey your law, for ever and ever. I will walk about in freedom, for I have sought out your precepts" (Ps. 119:44–45).

Teaching our children biblical concepts of authority is a huge task. This is not a single lesson in devotions one night, but a daily activity in which we lovingly teach biblical hierarchy to our children. Ephesians 6:1–3 is a passage written to children.

> Children, obey your parents in the Lord, for this is right. "Honor your father and your mother"—which is the first commandment with a promise—"that it may go well with you and that you may enjoy long life on the earth."

You could have this conversation with your children: "God has drawn a circle (see illustration on page 83) in which children are to live. God, who is good and kind, who has made you and all things for his own glory, who freely gives us every good gift, has given you a mother and a father who are wise, who are mature, and who have life experience. It is a good thing for you to obey Mommy and Daddy."

Rich Rewards for Obedience Promised in Ephesians 6

Let's look more closely at the expressions *obedience, honor, it will go well,* and *long life.*

Obedience

Obedience is submission to God's authority. Submission is Godward in its focus. We obey because there is a God in heaven. Obedience is submission to God's authority that causes a child to do what he is told to do, without arguing, without stalling, and without challenging.

do what you're told

When a child is arguing about whether it is legitimate for a parent to make a request, that child is not submitting. If that child has to be "sold" on what must be done, there is no true submission.

When a child delays obedience or responds when convenient, there is no submission. That child is acting independently. The effect is, "I will obey you on my timetable, not on yours."

When a child is challenging a parent's authority, or asking why in a demanding tone, that child is not submitting. Submission means responding to God's authority by cheerfully doing whatever is required.

Honor

Honor is a response to God's authority (the focus is always Godward) that causes a child to speak to his parents in a manner that shows respect for their role as God's agent of discipline and correction.

Present your authority in ways that are wise and kind. Biblical submission is never taught by coming to children in a demanding tone asserting, "Look here, I put a roof over your head, I buy every stitch of clothes on your back, every morsel of food that goes into your mouth, and as long as you live in my house you're going to do as I say."

If you come to your children with a presentation that asserts your power because you are the provider, you are planting seeds of rebellion. There is a good possibility that eventually your child will reject your authority. If you think about it, he will be rejecting a presentation that is not rooted in a biblical view of the world, but in your assertion of power because you are the provider. You have not presented God as the one who called for submission; you have only sought to leverage your provision as a parent into a demand for obedience.

Remind your children that God calls them to obey and promises rich blessings as they follow his ways. He promises, "Honor your father and your mother, so that you may live long in the land the Lord your God is giving you" (Ex 20:12). It is sweet and seemly for parents to rule and for children to submit. The circle of Ephesians 6 is a circle of blessing.

Children should not speak to parents as though they were peers. They must not speak in a challenging and disrespectful tone. They should not give mommy and daddy commands. They must speak in ways that show respect for the fact that God has placed their parents in authority. We commonly hear children of all ages say things to their parents that are so unkind and ungracious that it would not even be proper to address a peer in that way.

Joyful submission to God's authority creates a culture that is whole and biblical. Culture tells people how to think about each other and how to act toward each other. Our rebellious and disobedient culture is accurately reflected in the disrespectful manner in which children speak to their parents. We cannot begin with the proper behaviors; we must build a foundation of Christian thought about authority. Proper ways of speaking and responding will follow. An important part of that foundation is teaching our children that the world is vertical for parents and children—not horizontal.

God has designed children to be under parental authority because he is kind and loving. He has provided loving parents to watch over them as they grow. Parents have wisdom, maturity, and life experience. Children then enjoy protection and direction as they learn about themselves and the world in which they live. In God's abundant kindness he promises wonderful blessings as children honor and obey Mom and Dad.

It Will Go Well for You

There are innumerable spiritual blessings for children who live under God's structures of authority. They learn that God is good and kind. They learn that creatures find happiness as they know and trust God. They understand that the true nature of freedom is not autonomy (being a law to myself), but joyfully walking in God's laws. They learn to trust God to work through their parents to bring blessing to their lives. They learn that true joy is not having my own way, but following the will of God. They learn that living as God has ordained is the best life a created being can have.

These are rich spiritual blessings. Children will never learn these truths if they are self-directed, autonomous people who think life is good only when they have no external restraints.

There are also practical ways it goes well with obedient children. People respond much more favorably to children who are under authority than to children who are wild and unruly.

Imagine planning a family outing with your children. You are going to spend the day hiking through some rugged and beautiful country and perhaps enjoy an overnight under the stars. You want to invite one or two other children along to be companions and to enjoy the adventure with your family. Who are you going to invite? A child who is wild and unruly? A child who will only listen to you if he happens to agree? A child who will complain when the firewood needs to be gathered? A child who will fight you over each step of the hike? You get the point. You are going to invite a child who is responsive to adult leadership. In scores of practical ways it will go well with the child who understands that God's world is vertical.

The world doesn't cease to be vertical because we think it is horizontal. We cannot change the ways that God has made the world. I can refuse to acknowledge God's orderly maintenance of the atmosphere through what we call gravitation, but if I walk off the top of a tall building, gravity will be authenticated immediately.

You Will Enjoy Long Life

As children live under authority, God promises long life (Eph. 6:1–3). We all know that God takes some children when they are very young. These deaths seem tragic and untimely to us, but we believe in the kind providence of God who is good even when it is beyond our understanding. The general biblical principle is that God promises fullness of life to children who submit to God's structures of authority.

Why This Is So Important

Teaching these things to our children reminds them that creatures find their greatest joys and happiness in following God's ways. Human beings are made for God. All of God's laws are fully coordinated with the way we are designed. Many Christians live as though the greatest delights are found in the world, and that we have to deny ourselves those joys. God seems, to them, to stand for a rigid, dour life of denial and the world stands for joys and delights that God has denied to us. Not true. Rather, God shares with us his river of delights, eternal joys found only in him. If we taste and see, we will find the Lord is good.

Christian living does involve self-denial. God calls us to avoid all that is destructive. Such self-denial assures a deeper and more satisfying experience of those delights for which we are made. Remember the locomotive (see sidebar). Things don't start going well when it leaves the track; things grind to a halt.

> Here is a way to describe to your children the importance of boundaries and the freedom that they create. Imagine that I observe a sixty-ton locomotive running along the tracks and think to myself, "Look at that powerful locomotive with so much potential. What a shame that it is restricted to the confines of the tracks. Let's set the locomotive free and allow it to run across the meadow, through the woods, or wherever it would like to go." How free would the locomotive be? It would quickly become mired in the soft ground of the meadow. The locomotive is free on the tracks. God has laid the tracks for us. You and your children will find the greatest freedom and enjoyment in running freely along those tracks.

Danger of Being a Fool

The alternative to teaching our children biblical hierarchy is to allow them to be autonomous self-directed people. The Bible has a term for such a person: the fool. "The fool says in his heart, 'There is no God'" (Ps. 14:1). The fool says, "I will be my own self-directed person; no one will tell me what to do. I will do what I want to do, when I want to do it. I will be ruled by nothing other than my own whim." This is not freedom; it is foolishness. To live in God's world as though there is no God is the height of folly. A later chapter will be devoted to the contrast between wisdom and folly.

Our Lives Must Reflect the Truths We Teach

These truths must be reflected in our entertainment choices. The man in the action-adventure movie who does whatever he wants and breaks all the rules is not a hero. He is a fool. Regardless of the apparent good that results in the end, he is a fool and the world he represents is a lie. It wouldn't be wise to make an evening's entertainment of watching powerful dramas that teach our children to think about life in ways that are not true. If we are going to watch an action-adventure movie, we should have some vigorous discussion afterward about the fact that this hero is, according to the Bible's reckoning, a fool.

These truths must be consistently reflected in our lives. We cannot teach kids to respect our authority and then call our boss disrespectful names. Our children will not respect the spiritual authority of the church if we have roasted preacher for lunch on the Lord's Day. They will not be grateful for civil authority if we have no concern for civil servants or the traffic laws.

We can share our struggles with authority with our children. It is not hypocritical to ask our children to do things we struggle with doing. It *is* hypocritical to pretend that we do not struggle. We should show them grace and strength from God for their struggles by modeling humble dependence on God for our struggles.

Helping Children Evaluate Themselves

Proverbs 9 will help our children evaluate themselves, "Whoever corrects a mocker invites insult; whoever rebukes a wicked man incurs abuse. Do not rebuke a mocker or he will hate you; rebuke a wise man and he will love you. Instruct a wise man and he will be wiser still; teach a righteous man and he will add to his learning" (Prov. 9:7–9).

We used this passage to help our children evaluate their responses to parental authority. I would draw a stick figure of myself. I would ask, "What four words in this passage describe the communication of the parent?" They would search the passage and discover these four words, "Correct, rebuke, instruct, and teach."

"Wonderful! You guys are so smart. This next question will be really hard, but I think you can do it. The passage describes two different people responding to correction, rebuke, instruction, and teaching and it gives two names for each one. Can you find the names in the passage?"

They would look and look and maybe even need some hints, but eventually they would say, "One is a mocker or a wicked man and the other is a wise man or a righteous man."

I would draw two children on my paper and we would label one *mocker/wicked* and we would label the other *wise/righteous*. I would ask them, "How does this passage say the *mocker/wicked* responds to correction, rebuke, instruction, and teaching?"

They would look through the passage and find the answer. "He insults, abuses, and hates the person who corrects him."

"Very good, now see if you can find how the *wise/righteous* responds." Again they would look and uncover the answer.

"He loves, he grows wiser, and he adds to his learning." Then we would ask them for some self-evaluation.

"Which do you think you are being right now? Are you responding to Mommy and Daddy as a *wise/righteous* son or as a *mocker/wicked* son? How do you think you usually respond? How would your friends characterize your responses?

"You know something? Neither you nor Mom or Dad are always 100 percent right in our responses. We fail. Sometimes, Mom or Dad responds in ways that are foolish. But we know where to go with that, don't we? We can find forgiveness and change and power from Jesus."

We cannot overestimate the value of this kind of shepherding. We are coming alongside our children, identifying with their weaknesses, and leading them to know the power of grace.

Appealing to Authorities

When our children have embraced parental authority as God's purpose to do them good, it is important to teach them how to appeal to their authorities.[5] Parents are not always fair. Sometimes they are arbitrary and capricious. Our children live in a fallen world in which they will sometimes be wronged by authorities. If we teach them how to respectfully appeal, we will have equipped them to wisely interact with authority.

Growing into the Ability to Make Decisions

Some people object that children under authority will not learn to be decision-makers. The reasoning goes like this. How can they learn to make decisions if they never make decisions for themselves?

The best training for making decisions is to model for children good decision-making. Take them into your confidence. Share with them how mature people with biblical wisdom and insight make decisions. Share the patterns of reasoning and evaluation that you use to make decisions. Help them learn to avoid pressure from others, avoid responding emotionally, or making decisions without enough information.

Boundaries Versus Wisdom

We must teach our children to identify the difference between boundary issues and wisdom issues.[6] God has told us what we must do and what we must not do. Any command or prohibition is a boundary. There are also wisdom issues. The Bible does not have a direct precept regarding every particular choice a person may make, but the wisdom teachings of the Bible address most, if not all, issues.

If I am in a jewelry store looking at a fine wristwatch and the phone rings, distracting the clerk for a moment, I do not have to ask myself if I should steal the watch. That is a boundary issue. God says, "Thou shalt not steal." Stealing watches is always wrong. I may not transgress God's boundaries.

Should I buy the watch? That is a wisdom issue. There is no passage telling me to buy or not to buy the watch. But wisdom teaches me to ask thoughtful questions. Is this purchase a good stewardship of the money God has entrusted to me? Is the price a good price? Is it the kind of watch that I need? Can I afford this watch? At my age I might add, "Are the numbers large enough for me to see?" Each of these is a wisdom question. What may be an appropriate purchase at one time may not be at another time. What may be appropriate for one person may not be for another person. The boundary/wisdom question provides your children with a framework in which they can learn to make decisions.

Decision-makers with Advisors

My point is this. We must teach our children to be solid decision-makers by modeling good decision-making. Trial and error is not the best teacher. If trial and error was the best way to learn, instead of teaching wisdom to his son, Solomon could have just sent his son out into the world to blunder along, and saved his breath to cool his porridge.

not before? During the teenage years, it is appropriate to allow our children to make some decisions for themselves. But we must shepherd them through evaluating their choices. We may even let them think through the decision and then come for help to evaluate their thinking. Sometimes we will even let them make mistakes when the results will not be catastrophic. We have plenty of time to teach our children to be decision-makers. They will be better decision-makers if they have learned to be people under authority.

Christ Is Our Supreme Example of Submission

Formative instruction about authority corrects the prevailing culture's lies about autonomy. Teach and model this truth for your children, while you're out on a hike, riding in the van, getting ready for bed—all the time.

Christ is a wonderful example for our children. He humbled himself. He placed himself under authority. Christ submitted to the Father for the purpose of redemption. He came to earth on the Father's mission. He spoke the words the Father gave him to say. He always did the things that the Father told him to do. He was fully submissive to his father.

His subordination to the Father was not because he was inferior. He is equal to the Father in every way. He could have demanded the recognition that was his due. It would not have been usurpation. Instead, he placed himself under authority in order to provide redemption for us.

He is our model. He is the one who empowers our submission and makes it joyful and good. Delighting in him enables us to see that it is sweet and seemly to joyfully take our roles.

CHAPTER 8

Giving Children a Vision
for the Glory of God

We Are Worshipers

Children are instinctively worshipers. They are glory givers. It isn't a conscious decision on their part; they are hard-wired for worship. This chapter is about teaching our kids to see the *glory* of God and respond in worship.

You may be thinking, "Not my kids, they fall asleep in church." Be that as it may, they are worshipers. They are made in the image of God. They are uniquely designed for worship. Their eyes and ears and imaginations are receptors for seeing the glory of God in all that he has made so they can respond with worship, adoration, and love.

Your children go into the world everyday in search of an answer to the question, "What makes life worth living? What can I find to excite and delight me?" We do not have to look far; the world conspires to seduce the heart with cheap and empty pleasures.

God designed children for worship. The only question is, what will they worship? Romans 1:19–20 says God is revealed in his creation. His glory is seen through what he has made so that mankind—children—are without excuse. The physical world showcases the artistic creativity, endless power, and manifold wisdom of its Creator, so that we might find eternal joy in his glorious goodness.

What will they worship?

93

What happens when creatures uniquely designed to be dazzled by God's greatness and respond with worship, fail to worship God?

They do not cease worship; they simply worship something other than God.

we always worship

> For although they knew God, they neither glorified him as God nor gave thanks to him, but their thinking became futile and their foolish hearts were darkened. Although they claimed to be wise, they became fools and exchanged the glory of the immortal God for images made to look like mortal man and birds and animals and reptiles.
>
> —Romans 1:21–23

The key word here is "exchange." They exchanged the glory of God for the worship of created things. The same truth is repeated in Romans 1:25, "They exchanged the truth of God for a lie, and worshiped and served created things rather than the Creator—who is forever praised."

Created for Amazement

Kids love to be amazed. That is why we enjoy watching sports on TV. We love to marvel at amazing feats that ordinary mortals cannot accomplish. Whether football, basketball, ice skating or skiing, we love to be dazzled by athleticism.

This is uniquely human. There are no diving competitions for penguins in the Antarctic. They dive from massive ice flows, barely breaking the water, and yet no one scores them. At the end of the day there is no award ceremony.

A brown bear grabs a salmon from the raging Columbia River. No bears line the shores applauding. Little bears don't idolize Big Brown. They don't hang posters of him in their dens.

Idolizing greatness is innately human. We are made in the image of God and engineered for worship. We are fashioned for the fascination his glory evokes. Worship is a response to greatness.

Idols of the Heart

Your children will worship God or idols. The idols are not small statues; they are more subtle than that. Ezekiel 14:2–3 paints the vivid picture of God's people setting up idols in their hearts. The heart becomes a shrine where idols are worshiped.

We think of idol worshipers as unsophisticated primitive people or those involved in grievous sins. In the Bible, idolatry is the most frequent metaphor for loving created things more than God. Strive to understand idols of the heart. You will learn to detect your own idolatry and to talk to your children about their idols. Paul makes it clear in Ephesians 5:5 and Colossians 3:5 that idolatry is not a marginal footnote in life. Rather, the idolatry of greed, lust, craving, and coveting often dominate life.

Below is a suggestive list of idols of heart.

POWER AND INFLUENCE

Perhaps your child wants to control people. A girl in our Christian school came to school as a five-year-old CEO. If permitted, she would select the recess games each day and be the self-appointed coach, referee, line judge and statistician.

She would announce the dress code, "Tomorrow, we are all wearing jumpers." Heaven help the girl who showed up the next day with pants! She had a clear capacity to draw from others a desire to please her.

PRIDE AND PERFORMANCE

Perhaps your child is only happy if he can excel—run faster, jump higher, or spell better than others. The ticket price for center stage is never too high. They will sacrifice, they will deny themselves, they will practice; they will do whatever it takes.

For these children, to have the highest test score, to win the race, to develop virtuosity, is to be whole. When they fail to obtain these distinctions, they are disconsolate. Nothing can cheer them, not even God and his sovereign purposes.

Parents and teachers miss these idols because a driven child is not a management problem. In fact, adults polish this idol. We like it when our children excel. I can almost hear someone ask, "What's wrong with excelling?" Think about this. *The person who has God plus every imaginable skill and ability has no more than the person who has only God.*

Children who are driven to perform crave praise. Praise from others completes the joy of performance. The roar of the crowd at the winning field goal is sweeter than a dozen field goals alone on the practice field. Performance driven children are usually addicted to praise.

POSSESSIONS

Some children are possessive of their things. They get miffed if something of theirs is damaged. They are reluctant to lend their "stuff."

They will pour over catalogs that come to your house. They show you the catalog pictures to regale you with neat stuff to buy. They envy what others have. When they leave the house they look for assurances that no one will touch their stuff while they are gone.

PLEASURE AND SENSUALITY

Some children love the rush of going places and doing things. Life is good when there is something new and exciting to do or to see. They crave excitement. They love the rush of riding the bike off a ramp, racing down a ski slope, or driving their go-kart. They are always seeking some new sensation. Whenever there is no heart-throbbing, adrenaline-pumping activity to do, they are bored because there is nothing to do.

FEAR OF MAN OR THE DESIRE FOR APPROVAL

The fear of man and the desire to be approved by others are opposite sides of the same coin. What others will think of their shoes, their clothes, their hair or their ideas can be paralyzing for children. Teens ignore their own brothers or sisters out of embarrassment because they yearn for approval from peers. They will do wrong rather than be uncool. They are addicted to the attention of others, even if it is negative attention.

FRIENDSHIP

Often friendship becomes the badge of worth for children. Their loyalty to peers may be greater than loyalty to parents. They would deceive mom or dad more quickly than "rat out" a friend. The normal ebb and flow of relationships can produce wild mood swings as well as mistrust between teens and parents.

BEING "IN THE KNOW"

Somewhat related is the passion some children have for being "in the know." Knowing the latest movie, music CD or video game is a solemn duty. They will "fake it" in a conversation where they don't know the latest and greatest. They have eyes for the most trendy clothes, phrases, attitudes or icons. If they are nothing else, they are hip.

Idols Don't Satisfy

We could multiply illustrations. The whole world could not satisfy the void in the heart. Only God, who has made our hearts his home, can fully and completely satisfy.

Either your children will love and serve God or exchange the truth of God for a lie and worship and serve created things rather than the Creator. Teach them to understand the heart's propensity to manufacture idols.

When you think of idols of the heart, don't think of scandalous sins. Think of harmless hobbies in which children will invest vast amounts of time. Think of the daydreams that provide excitement to a heart that is not finding true and lasting pleasures in knowing God.

Helping Kids See the Glory of God

Idols of the heart lose their grip on the soul when they are replaced by greater, more pleasing delights. Your children are hard-wired for delights that last, not for a moment, but for a lifetime and for eternity.

Because your children are uniquely designed to worship God, one of your most important callings is to display the glory of God. Your job is to help your children see the dazzling excellence of God. Children will never have right thoughts about themselves until they have right thoughts about God.

Our call: to display the glory of God

Psalm 145 uses rich language to describe this essential instruction. It describes your most important job as a parent when it says, "One generation will commend your works to another; they will tell of your mighty acts. They will speak of the glorious splendor of your majesty . . . They will tell of the power of your awesome works . . . They will celebrate your abundant goodness and joyfully sing of your righteousness" (Ps. 145:4–7). This sums up parenting. Commend the works of God.

The deepest, most profound joys are found in knowing God. Children's deceitful hearts will tell them that life is found in other places. Formative instruction unveils the beauty of God. There is a resplendent radiance to the power and personality of God. The glory of God demonstrates that he is praiseworthy. God's character gives a reason for hope and confidence. He is worthy of our trust, praise and boasting.

do I communicate this to my kids?

God's Glory in the Psalms

Let us take on a fast survey of several Psalms that display God's glory in particular circumstances. Your child feels that everything is going wrong. Nothing is going his way! He is asking the question of Psalm 4:6–7.

> Many are asking, "Who can show us any good?"
>   Let the light of your face shine on us, O LORD.
> You have filled my heart with greater joy
>   than when their grain and new wine abound.

What will help your child in his discouragement?

Note the word picture here. *"Let the light of your face shine on us, O Lord,"* is a beautiful metaphor for the delight of the nearness of God. It is more joyous than an abundant harvest when grain and new wine abound.

Let this word picture sink in. David was writing in a technologically simple age with no science of food preservation. There were no greenhouses to extend the harvest. The harvest would spoil if not eaten. The metaphor is made more intense when we think of the toil of tilling, planting, cultivating, and gathering a harvest. Can you imagine the joy of harvest?

Bring this metaphor to life for your downhearted children. "Children, when everything is going wrong, when you feel like no one is on your side, remember David's answer to the same question. The greatest joys you can know are found in savoring the presence of God."

Your children are trying to satisfy their appetites in lesser joys. You and I do it, too. Have you found yourself tired, out of sorts, feeling on edge, standing at the open refrigerator door? What are you doing? You have already eaten. You are looking for comfort in some left-over fried chicken or a bowl of ice cream. Your children are casting about, looking for something to take the edge off their restlessness.

Oh, that we would live in the light of God's glorious presence. Draw near in prayer. Meditate on his goodness. Delight in him and he will give greater joy than grain and new wine (or even a bag of potato chips). Eternal pleasures are found in God.

> Keep me safe, O God,
>   for in you I take refuge.
> I said to the LORD, "You are my Lord;
>   apart from you I have no good thing."
>
> —Psalm 16:1–2

> Lord, you have assigned me my portion and my cup;
>> you have made my lot secure.
> The boundary lines have fallen for me in pleasant places;
>> surely I have a delightful inheritance (Ps. 16:5–6).
> Therefore my heart is glad and my tongue rejoices;
>> my body also will rest secure (Ps. 16:9).
> You have made known to me the path of life;
>> you will fill me with joy in your presence,
>> with eternal pleasures at your right hand (Ps. 16:11).

Point your children to God as the fountain of deepest pleasure. In his presence are eternal pleasures—the greatest beauty, the highest value, the deepest satisfaction, the longest lasting joy, the most satisfying delights, the most wonderful friendship—eternal pleasures are found in God.

Say every day, "I can show you the path of life. I can show you where your heart can be filled with joy. You can enter into pleasures of knowing and delighting in God that will never be exhausted; these pleasures will continue to provide joy for eternity." Is this Psalm your hope in fear and uncertainty? Model it for your children.

Eternal pleasures of delight in God will continue into eternity. Throughout the coming ages God will disclose more and more of the unsearchable riches of his goodness (Eph. 2:7). Every day there will be new episodes of God's glory. We will never be bored because we will always be finite creatures being dazzled by the glories of an infinite God.

This formative instruction really "goes with the grain" of your children's needs. Hold out the glories and excellence of the living God. Their hearts will be strengthened and sustained by knowing a really big and beautiful God. Make mental note of the ways they yearn for pleasure and delight. Look for opportunities to direct them to eternal pleasures.

Everything today comes "satisfaction guaranteed," but little satisfies. For all who delight in God, life only heightens the sense of satisfaction they will know in the presence of God. Show your children the beauties of the One who satisfies.

> The LORD is my light and my salvation—
>> whom shall I fear?
> The LORD is the stronghold of my life—
>> of whom shall I be afraid?
> When evil men advance against me
>> to devour my flesh,

> when my enemies and foes attack me,
>   they will stumble and fall.
> Though an army besiege me,
>   my heart will not fear;
> though war break out against me,
>   even then I will be confident.
> One thing I ask of the LORD,
>   and this is what I seek:
> that I may dwell in the house of the LORD
>   all the days of my life,
> to gaze upon the beauty of the LORD
>   and to seek him in his temple.
>
> —Psalm 27:1–4

This is a Psalm of siege. In this Psalm, evil men, enemies, foes, even armies are against the psalmist. He has one request of God. Amazingly, he does not request deliverance from the enemies. Rather, he asks for the nearness of God. He longs to gaze on the beauty of the Lord, to seek him, to know him as a shelter, to sing and make music to the Lord.

David's greatest deliverance is spiritual, not physical. When things are spinning out of control, God's presence brings deliverance.

Your children sometimes face difficulties—mockery, taunting, and cruelty from other children. Your child's profoundest need in those dark times is to find shelter in God. These are opportunities to describe the comfort of God's love and care to your children.

Remind your children, who are instinctively worshipers, that there is a glorious God whose love is better than life.

> Your love, O LORD, reaches to the heavens,
>   your faithfulness to the skies.
> Your righteousness is like the mighty mountains,
>   your justice like the great deep.
>
> —Psalm 36:5–6

The psalmist uses the immense creation to describe attributes of God. God's love and faithfulness are as vast as the universe. His righteousness is high and lofty like the Himalayas. God's justice is deep like the ocean. What vivid and graphic pictures of the greatness and glory of God! Talk about the greatness and glory of God using these pictures.

The physical world exists to display the unending power and multifaceted wisdom and external greatness of its creator, the Lord

Jesus Christ. The creation displays the eternal qualities of God. He created a world with mountains, forests, vineyards, fields, pastures, deserts, gates, roads, paths, fountains, springs, pools, streams, rivers, and oceans so that you can use tangible pictures to teach your children God's goodness. He designed relationships—kings, subjects, rulers, nations, families, fathers, mothers, sisters, brothers, children, husbands, and wives—so that we could understand God as one who is wise and good. He made seasons—seedtime, harvest, cold, heat, spring, clouds, rain, summer, fall, winter, and even snow to display faithfulness. God furnished the world with buildings, houses, doors, temples and palaces so we could know of his provision for our every need. He gave trees that blossom and bear fruit, gardens of flowers that bloom and fade, grass to flourish and be mowed down, sheep and shepherds, bears and cubs in order to reveal his infinity and our finitude. The sun, moon and starry hosts tell about his eternal power and divine nature. Even our bodies with heads, hands, feet, eyes to see, mouths to speak and ears to hear are all designed to display the excellence of God. Everything he has made—banquets, lamps, darkness, weeping, laughter, treasures of gold, silver, rubies and everything else God has made is uniquely designed to declare the wisdom, goodness, creativity and magnanimity of a sovereign God.

You can easily get from anything in the creation to conversation about the goodness and grandeur of God. Daily living is a series of opportunities to talk about the glory of God.

David continues in Psalm 36,

> O LORD, you preserve both man and beast.
>   How priceless is your unfailing love!
> Both high and low among men
>   find refuge in the shadow of your wings.
> They feast on the abundance of your house;
>   you give them drink from your river of delights.
> For with you is the fountain of life;
>   in your light we see light.
>
> —Psalm 36:6b–9

You and your children are invited to the spiritual delicacies that God offers. Drink deeply from his river of delights. Immerse yourselves in this fountain that will never run dry.

You have the privilege of saying, "Children, there is an abundant Christ who can quench the thirst of your soul. You were made for him. Don't exchange the truth for a lie. Worship and serve the Creator, not created things."

God's love is better than life.

> O God, you are my God, earnestly I seek you;
>> my soul thirsts for you, my body longs for you,
>> in a dry and weary land where there is no water.
> I have seen you in the sanctuary
>> and beheld your power and your glory.
> Because your love is better than life,
>> my lips will glorify you.
> I will praise you as long as I live,
>> and in your name I will lift up my hands.
> My soul will be satisfied, as with the richest of foods;
>> with singing lips my mouth will praise you.
>
> —Psalm 63:1–5

Delighting in God restores your sense of what is ultimately valuable. Worship of God energizes you to seek joy and satisfaction in him alone. This world is fleeting and unworthy of your heart's devotion.

Delight in God awakens the soul; at the same time everything else in life that competes with God for your devotion fades. The heart that is delighting in the glory of God is inoculated against the noisy demands of the world.

Help your children delight in God. You may be thinking, "I wasn't looking for heavy theology; I was looking for practical child rearing advice." Remember this. Your children are not likely to grow into adults who truly know God unless you provide them with a big God who is worthy of worship.

What type of God do I portray?

John Bunyan longed for his family during his years of imprisonment for his faith. God showed him that, "Not only was God infinitely more satisfying than worldly pleasures; he was more satisfying than even the sacred pleasures of home and family. The pleasures of life are fleeting, but the love of God is better than life itself."

Describe God's character, his mighty deeds and the soul-satisfying joys of knowing him, reminding them, "Children, your souls are looking for satisfaction and it is only found in God." Asaph says in Psalm 73:25–26:

Whom have I in heaven but you?
And being with you, I desire nothing on earth.
My flesh and my heart may fail,
but God is the strength of my heart
and my portion forever.

If you want your children to have a reason to sing on Sunday, give
them a glorious God. If you want your children to have a reason not
to sin on Monday, give them a glorious God. If you want them to
think of nobler things than the latest, mind-numbing video fantasy
game, give them a glorious God. If you want them to dream grander
dreams than illicit sex or more money or more stuff, give them a glorious God. If you want them to have a reason for confidence when
life seems to spin out of control, give them a glorious God.

Give my kids a glorious God.

When friends are offering the pleasures of sin for a season, they
need a glorious God. Godly fear—that sense of awe and reverence
that inspires true worship—requires a glorious God. God is the one
before whom they should tremble and worship with reverence and
awe. The glory of God will stoke the fires of true worship and godly
living.

Where will the human hunger be satisfied? Rest in God alone. Isn't
it amazing that Christ sacrificed himself for you and me? Lasting
happiness is found in making much of God for eternity. There is a
transcendent satisfaction in God which trials and difficulties cannot
diminish and which success and pleasure cannot enhance.

The Heart of the Gospel Is the Glory of God

We live in perilous times. Modern evangelism has reduced the
message and purpose of the gospel. Much of evangelical Christian-
ity is focused on getting people to pray the sinner's prayer so that
they can go to heaven. The heart of the gospel is the glory of God.
God is so jealous for his own glory that he sent his Son to redeem
broken, sinful, unworthy people (Isa. 42:8). The Son prayed that his
followers would see his glory (Jn. 17:24). The glory of God moved
his holy heart to choose a people (Rom. 9:23).

God extends grace to broken people for his own glory. God is
glorified when he is treasured above all, when he is your greatest
prize, when he is your fountain of delight.

Consider Psalm 96:1–3:

> Sing to the LORD a new song;
>   sing to the LORD, all the earth.
> Sing to the LORD, praise his name;
>   proclaim his salvation day after day.
> Declare *his glory* among the nations,
>   his marvelous deeds among all peoples.

The proclamation of salvation is a proclamation of the glory of God. The heart of the gospel is the glory of God. He is great and greatly to be praised. He is to be feared above all gods. Splendor, glory, and majesty are his. He reigns.

God does not exist for man; man exists for God. Jesus Christ restores broken, fallen man to a true worship of God. The God of the Bible is the supreme object of worship. Jesus Christ saves sinners and makes them worshipers.

The Treasure Principle

Matthew 13:44 (ESV) says, "The kingdom of heaven is like treasure hidden in a field, which a man found and covered up. Then in his joy he goes and sells all that he has and buys that field."

The man found a treasure. He buried it again. He hoped no one saw it. Filled with joy, he went off and sold everything so that he could buy the field and possess the treasure. He did not sell all out of a sense of duty. Can you imagine finding the treasure and saying, "Wouldn't you know that I would have to find the treasure in the field? I hate it when this happens to me! Now I will have to sell all my stuff so I can buy that stupid field and possess that treasure." He didn't divest of his possessions out of a sense of duty. He sold out of a sense of profound joy. The treasure dazzled him.

This is what the kingdom of heaven is like. Until your children have understood that it is worthwhile to divest of everything, that nothing in all the earth matters but knowing and loving Jesus, they will never know him and love him and serve him. Delight in God cannot occur in a vacuum. Display and demonstrate the wonders of God.

Your Children Are Thirsty

> Come, all you who are thirsty,
>   come to the waters;
> and you who have no money,
>   come, buy and eat!

> Come buy wine and milk
>> without money and without cost.
> Why spend money on what is not bread,
>> and your labor on what does not satisfy?
> Listen, listen to me, and eat what is good,
>> and your soul will delight in the richest of fare.
> Give ear and come to me;
>> hear me that your soul may live.
>
> —Isaiah 55:1–3

Your children are uniquely designed for worship. They have thirsty souls. Show them where you find living water. Remember Jesus' words, "If a man is thirsty, let him come to me and drink. Who believes in me, as the Scripture has said, streams of living water will flow from within him" (Jn. 7:37–38). Most drinks are consumed in the drinking, but this drink becomes a fountain within.

Why Is this so Important?

Implication 1: Interpretation Is Everything

Children interpret everything that happens to them. Their interpretation of circumstances determines how they will respond. The key to interpreting life is the glory of God. Children who are dazzled by the Lord of glory will interpret the experiences and opportunities of life correctly. The primary truth of all interpretation is the being and existence and glory of the God of the Bible.

Isaiah 40 is God's comfort for his people in captivity. It declares the power and immensity of God. He is the God who scoops up the ocean in the palm of his hand, who stretches out the heavens. He is the God before whom the nations are like grasshoppers, who calls the stars out by name and whose great power is the reason no stars are missing. He raises and deposes rulers and princes. So the prophet asks, "Why do you say, O Jacob, and complain, O Israel, 'My way is hidden from the Lord; my cause is disregarded by my God'? Do you not know? Have you not heard? The Lord is the everlasting God, the Creator of the ends of the earth. He will not grow tired or weary, and his understanding no one can fathom" (Isa. 40:27–28).

Israel needed to remember the glory of the creator and sustainer of the universe to interpret their circumstances correctly.

Implication 2: Children Sin for Pleasure

Tell your children that the pleasures of sin are fleeting. Solid joys and lasting pleasures come through knowing and loving God. As Augustine said, "We are made for God and we will be restless until we find our rest in him."

Implication 3: Don't Feed the Idols

I observe that many parents feed their children's idols. They take delight in their children's delight in possessions. They fill their lives with excitement and pleasures. Parents expend enormous amounts of time, money, and energy in the development of performance abilities. Families are so overcommitted to activities that there is precious little time for meals together, family devotions, or simple conversation and family enjoyment.

I have observed children coming to church in their Little League uniforms. At 11:55, the family quietly slips out of the Lord's Day worship service. The game starts at noon and the coach won't play anyone who is late. The church is gathered to exult in God's presence and to hear his Word. The pastor is opening the Word of God. Just as he is getting to application, an entire family leaves the church because there is something more time sensitive—the child's participation in Little League. If this child concludes that life is found in knowing God it will be in spite of, not because of, his parents' examples.

May God remove our blinders! There are scores of activities for children. While choosing from the dizzying array of choices, think carefully or you will inadvertently lead your children away from God rather than to him.

I am not against enjoying the blessings God has given us. To live in a home that is comfortable and nicely appointed, to provide your children dance lessons or sports opportunities is a blessing. If you can afford a piano and piano lessons, your children are blessed. I am not arguing for asceticism. But don't present a worldview in which life consists in these things, and God is just icing on the cake. God is the cake!

Implication 4: You Must Be Dazzled by God

Your children must see that you delight in God. If your children were asked, "What makes Dad or Mom tick?" their answer should be your love for God. Live so that your children are drawn into the presence of God.

Maurice Roberts writes, "Ecstasy and delight are essential to the believer's soul and they promote satisfaction. We were not meant to live without spiritual exhilaration, and the Christian who goes a long time without the experience of heart warming will soon find himself to be tempted to have his emotions satisfied from earthly things and not, as he ought, from the Spirit of God. The soul is so constituted that it craves fulfillment from things outside itself and will embrace earthly joys for satisfaction when it cannot reach spiritual ones . . . The believer is in spiritual danger if he allows himself to go for any length of time without tasting the love of Christ and savoring the felt comforts of the Savior's presence. When Christ ceases to fill the heart with satisfaction, our souls will go in silent search of other lovers"[7]

> Use a simple decision tree before enrolling your child in an activity. What will it cost? What is the commitment required? How many hours each week will we be "on call"? Does this activity conflict with things of higher priority (i.e. family worship, family meals, corporate worship at church)? What is the worldview of the coaches (i.e. language, values, view of the family)? How will this impact the rest of the family? Do the benefits outweigh the costs?

Implication 5: How Can You Obtain and Sustain a Vision for the Glory of God?

MEDITATE ON SPIRITUAL TRUTHS

Learn how to meditate on a passage of Scripture that describes the character and work of God. The Psalms and the Prophets are filled with passages that refresh your soul with wonderful pictures of God. Think about these character qualities in personal terms. If God is described as a father, think of him as your father—the consummate father. Meditate on all a good father does for his children. If he is described as a shelter, think of him as your shelter. Recognize the storms of life at this moment in your life and identify ways you can run into his shelter.

> How can you obtain and sustain a vision for the glory of God?
>
> 1. Meditate on spiritual truths.
> 2. Provide yourself with spiritual enticement.
> 3. Express your spiritual delights.

The more you meditate on God's attributes and his works, the more you will delight in him. Delighting in him will enlarge your capacity to trust him and rejoice in him. You are delighting in God when you can trust and rejoice in God when he is all you have. The person with everything plus God has no more than the person who has only God.

Provide Yourself with Spiritual Enticement

Use your driving times to sing along with hymns and Scripture songs. Listen to sermons and Christian audio books. Subscribe to an email daily devotional. Read Christian biographies that awaken spiritual appetites and strengthen holy longings. Provide yourself with continual exposure to holy aspirations.

Being dazzled by God will make you a better parent. Delight in God will dampen sin's effect on you. Prayer will become your first defense against temptation.

Express Your Spiritual Delights

Talk about your spiritual joys and triumphs. Even this will increase your longings for God. C. S. Lewis observed that praise not only expresses but actually completes the enjoyment of whatever is delightful to us.

Implication 6: Children and Young People Can "Get It"

Many Christians are cynical about whether their children can be moved by a vision for the glory of God. They can. They are made for this truth. It is the authentic answer to their deepest longings. It is self-authenticating truth. Your children can "get it."

I have had the joy of seeing young people in my family and in our church embrace these truths. I have met young people from all over the world who are inspired and thrilled by a delight in God's glory. Sadly, many youth ministries pander to the appetites in young people for the banality of the youth culture. Young people are idealistic and yearning for something grand and glorious that is worth living for.

Implication 7: Glory Is the Beginning and the End

The Christian life begins with the glory of God. Paul speaks in 2 Corinthians 4 about the god of this world blinding the minds of unbelievers so they cannot see the light of the gospel of the glory of Christ. In salvation, God does the same creative miracle that he did in creation. "For God, who said, 'Let light shine out of darkness,' made his light shine into our hearts to give us the light of the knowledge of the glory of God in the face of Christ" (2 Cor. 4:6). Christian life begins with glory.

Christian growth continues and progresses as we behold God's glory. "And we, who with unveiled faces all reflect [on] [contemplate, behold] the Lord's glory, are being transformed into his likeness with ever-increasing glory, which comes from the Lord, who is the Spirit" (2 Cor. 3:18). The more you are dazzled and entranced by God, the more like God you will become.

Turn yourself again to the one who saved you. Behold his glory that will transform you to his likeness. Your children will notice.

CHAPTER 9

Wisdom and Foolishness

I have a little game I play with my grandsons. I say, "You know, I believe you might not be a boy, you might be a monkey."

"No, Grandpa," they giggle, knowing what is coming. "I am a boy."

"Well, I don't know. You have two eyes like a monkey. You have two arms like a monkey. Let me see, you have two legs and every monkey I have ever seen had two legs. Yes, and you have hair on top of your head. You have two ears, one mouth, and one nose. I think you are a monkey; you resemble one in every way."

"But, Grandpa," they protest. "Monkeys have a tail and I don't have a tail."

"Oh, you're right, no tail. I guess you aren't a monkey after all."

Even children understand that sometimes the most effective way to distinguish between two things is by comparison. This chapter contrasts wisdom and foolishness.

The Biblical Understanding of Wisdom

Wisdom is the fear of the Lord. We are taught in Proverbs 9:10, "The fear of the LORD is the beginning of wisdom, and knowledge of the Holy One is understanding."

What is meant by "the fear of the Lord"? The fear of the Lord is reverence and awe of God. It is something young children can learn. When you talk about the fear of the Lord, be sure your children don't think about frightening movies or slavish fear. Recently, as I rode along with one of my five-year-old grandsons, he began talking to me about the fear of the Lord.

He said, "Grandpa, did you know that God is dangerous? My Papa told me that God is very powerful and he can do anything he wants to do. Nobody is strong enough to stop him. God is very dangerous. Papa said, 'He is good.' But he is very dangerous." This is the fear of the Lord for a kindergartner.

Our children will respond to life with wisdom when they reverence the Lord.

The Biblical Understanding of Foolishness

The Bible's definition of foolishness is concise. "The fool says in his heart, 'There is no God'" (Ps. 14:1). If there is no God, I am autonomous—a law unto myself. There is no consideration in life more profound than, "What will please me?"

Children don't say those words, but such foolish thoughts are the underlying justifications for hundreds of impulses every day. It is expressed in all the acts of disobedience, selfishness, willful temper, and compulsive self-love.

The Pursuits of Foolishness

Foolish human beings set out on a path to please themselves. How are their desires expressed?

(1) PLEASURE

The fool of Ecclesiastes 2, like the fools of our day, was a pleasure seeker. He said, "Come now, I will test you with pleasure to find out what is good. . . . I denied myself nothing my eyes desired; I refused my heart no pleasure" (Eccles. 2:1, 10). The attraction of pleasure is powerful in the life of a fool. This is the attraction of today's majority culture to our children.

I spoke recently to a high school teen. He said, "I just think this is the time of life to be wild and crazy." Sadly, he reflects the spirit of the age. Wild and crazy equals a good time.

Solomon, the author of Ecclesiastes, discovered the foolishness of pleasure:

"Laughter," I said, "is foolish. And what does pleasure
   accomplish?"
Sorrow is better than laughter, because a sad face is good for
   the heart.
Like the crackling of thorns under the pot, so is the laughter
   of fools.
This too is meaningless.

—Ecclesiastes 2:2; 7:3, 6

SUBSTANCES

Drugs and alcohol are shortcuts to sensual pleasure. The writer
of Ecclesiastes tried to find delight in mood altering substances. "I
tried cheering myself with wine" (Eccles. 2:3). Mind or mood altering substances provide a buzz, or hide youthful fears, or create an
escape from boredom. Our teens and even preteens are offered the
pleasures of a fool everywhere they look.

Children who say in their hearts, "There is no God," have no
internal resistance to the overtures of the fool. Wisdom brings
convictions.

Over a period of time, these substances that have been used for
pleasure become slavemasters. The person who indulges is no longer
free to make choices because they take over the individual's life.

SENSUALITY

The writer of Ecclesiastes knew how to party. He wrote, "I amassed
gold and silver for myself, and the treasure of kings and provinces. I
acquired men and women singers, and a harem as well—the delights
of the heart of man" (Eccles. 2:8). In the 1950s a foolish man developed a prurient magazine and set out a fantasy party life called the
playboy lifestyle. By the turn of the twenty-first century the spectacle
of this eighty-something man nightclubbing in Chicago with a bevy
of twenty-something women at his side has become respectable in
the eyes of the culture in which we are raising our children.

The fool who pursues sensuality will find himself driven by relent-
less cravings that cannot be fulfilled. The passion for pleasure requires
deeper and deeper sensual degradation to satisfy.

I denied myself nothing my eyes desired; I refused my heart no pleasure. . .Yet when I surveyed all that my hands had done and what I
had toiled to achieve, everything was meaningless, a chasing after the
wind; nothing was gained under the sun.

—Ecclesiastes 2:10–11

(4)   SUCCESS

Accomplishments

Some people define life in terms of success. The writer of Ecclesiastes understood the trap of being upwardly mobile. Today we might call him a successful developer. He writes, "I undertook great projects: I built houses for myself and planted vineyards. I made gardens and parks and planted all kinds of fruit trees in them. I made reservoirs to water groves of flourishing trees" (Eccles. 2:4–6). The goal of success is foolish without acknowledging God.

Children may think that joy will be found in accomplishment. They may devote themselves to success in school or sports and never achieve the satisfaction they desire. Later we will discuss how we have joy in accomplishments because our goal is to glorify God.

Wealth

The fool will find that even achieving a goal of financial success does not give satisfaction. We must remind our children that success measured by prosperity or possessions will always disappoint. The more we have, the more there is to worry about. "Whoever loves money never has money enough; whoever loves wealth is never satisfied with his income. This too is meaningless. As goods increase, so do those who consume them. And what benefit are they to the owner except to feast his eyes on them?" (Eccles. 5:10–11). "Wealth as an end for self-gratification is meaningless, but it can be a great blessing to the church and those in need" (1 Tim. 6:17–18).

The Preacher's Response from Ecclesiastes

The fool, whose goal is to be successful without remembering God, will not find satisfaction; he will find futility. This is the testimony of Ecclesiastes.

So I hated life, because the work that is done under the sun was grievous to me. All of it is meaningless, a chasing after the wind. I hated all the things I had toiled for under the sun, because I must leave them to the one who comes after me. And who knows whether he will be a wise man or a fool? Yet he will have control over all the work into which I have poured my effort and skill under the sun. This too is meaningless. So my heart began to despair over all my toilsome labor under the sun. For a man may do his work with wisdom, knowledge and skill, and then he must leave all he owns to someone who has not worked for it. This too is meaningless and a great misfortune. What does a man get for all the toil and anxious striving with which he labors under the sun? All his days his work is pain and grief; even at night his mind does not rest. This too is meaningless.

—Ecclesiastes 2:17–23

(5)   EDUCATION

Even education, as an end in itself, is a fool's pursuit. Remember, the fool is the one who lives as though there is no God. Education without reference to God is folly. As people who know God, we must understand why education is valuable. It will equip us to better serve God, as we will discuss further in this chapter.

Margy was doing some guidance interviews with junior high students from the Christian school. She asked the question, "Why learn?" Their answers expressed their limited understanding of the goal of education.

"So you can get into the best colleges."

"If you have a better education, you can get a better job."

"If I have a good education I will be able to make a lot of money."

Though these may be important steps for a young person to reach the goal of being prepared to serve God in adult life, none of them are sufficient goals themselves.

The writer of Ecclesiastes chose the path of education. He says, "I devoted myself to study and to explore by wisdom all that is done under heaven" (Eccles. 1:13).

The majority culture places great faith in education. The culture seems to think it is the answer to all troublesome problems. Millions are spent on drug education programs while the problems of drug addiction grow. Much is spent on sex education, but education fails to stem the tide of STDs, teen pregnancy, or abortion.

Information cannot cure the sickness of the human soul or satisfy the longings of our hearts. Education does not give life meaning and purpose.

The Outcome of a Life of Foolishness

Ignorance of academic information is not our greatest enemy; rebellion is. The fool's problem is not an information deficit; it is rebellion. People rebel by actively or passively refusing to recognize God's authority. Romans 1:28 says, "Since they did not see fit to acknowledge God, God gave them up to a debased mind to do what ought not to be done." The more education a fool receives, the more sophisticated and cunning his foolishness is. Academic education informs the mind, but has no power to purify the heart or to stem the tide of rebellion against God (see Rom. 1:18ff).

Pursuit of a Life of Wisdom

The fear of the Lord recognizes that God is ultimate. He is all that really matters. It is the wonder of being in his majestic presence and knowing that you are accepted in the beloved. No wonder the Psalmist said, "If you, O Lord, kept a record of sins, O Lord, who could stand? But with you there is forgiveness; therefore you are feared" (Ps. 130:3–4). John Newton wrote in *Amazing Grace*, "Twas grace that taught my heart to fear, and grace my fears relieved."

The fear of the Lord is a response to his holiness and his hatred of wickedness. Those who fear also know that God is awesome and glorious. Fear is the sense of reverential awe before his sovereign grandeur. It is also the awareness that along with his hatred for sin, he is determined to forgive and purge evil with lovingkindness.

How does a child learn the fear of the Lord? To answer that question, let me ask another. What would my children do if they knew there was hidden treasure in the back yard? They would dig up every square inch of the yard to find the treasure. Learning to fear the Lord comes through searching as one would search for hidden treasure. God will not hide himself from those who earnestly seek him.

Only God can ultimately draw our children to himself. God is the one who will convince them of truth, so they love him and fear him, in spite of the loud attractions of foolishness around them. Our instruction as parents, grandparents, and teachers is one of the means he uses (Deut. 4:10). Another means is our faithful and continuous prayers for our young people (Col. 1:9–14).

The Blessings of a Life of Wisdom

The Blessing of Understanding

The fear of the Lord produces understanding. The Psalms say, "The fear of the Lord is *the beginning* of wisdom; all who follow his precepts have good understanding" (Ps. 111:10). This is in contrast to the fool, who lacks understanding. Proverbs 13:20 says, "He who walks with the wise grows wise, but a companion of fools suffers harm." He suffers harm through his complicity with fools, but he cries, "It's not fair." Good sense and discernment are the blessings of those who fear the Lord.

The Blessing of Long Life

The fear of the Lord adds length of days. There is a young man in our church who lived many years as a prodigal in a far country before returning to the Father's house. He has attended more funerals of his peers than I have, even though I am thirty-five years his senior. People who live profligate lives do not live to old age. Solomon was grooming his son to be king. He warned, "The fear of the Lord adds length to life, but the years of the wicked are cut short" (Prov. 10:27).

The Blessing of Godly Values

The fear of the Lord realigns values. Our culture is like a department store in which some mischievous person has changed all the price tags. Fine watches are priced like inexpensive combs and expensive suits sell for less than neckties. A person's character is valued less than appearance, and kindness to others is valued less than a new car. But a person who fears the Lord learns to live with true values in life.

The Blessing of Moral Sensitivity

The fear of the Lord produces moral awareness. Those who pursue wisdom will be asking profound questions about life. Their personal standards and convictions will exceed "what will give pleasure for the moment." Proverbs 15 puts it this way, "Better a little with the fear of the Lord" (Prov. 15:16).

The Blessing of Honor

The fear of the Lord brings true honor. Children want to be noticed. They want approval. Often choices of clothing and other ways they adorn themselves are expressions of their desire for recognition, which is part of the image of God in man. The Proverbs speak to issues of honor and recognition with such poignancy. "The fear of the Lord teaches a man wisdom, and humility comes before honor" (Prov. 15:33). "Humility and the fear of the Lord bring wealth and honor and life" (Prov. 22:4).

Young people many times are focused on their present lives, and need encouragement to build for the future. The importance of the

It is good to read the Proverbs as a family each day. It was our habit to read the Proverbs every morning at the breakfast table. We read the number of the chapter in Proverbs that matched the day of the month. I then asked each of the children which particular proverb in the chapter caught their attention.

During their college years our son and daughter were working an afternoon shift together in a factory. Margy and I came home and found the Proverbs open on the dining table. They had been reading a chapter to each other before they left for work. As adults, it is still their habit to read the Proverbs daily. The truths they heard again and again have become a part of their thinking.

future includes this present world—their adult life, as well as eternal life (Rom. 2:7).

The Blessing of Eternal Joy

The human soul was created for infinite and eternal joys. "He has made everything beautiful in its time. He has also set eternity in the hearts of men; yet they cannot fathom what God has done from beginning to end" (Eccles. 3:11). God has placed an appetite for the eternal in the heart of man. Psalm 16:11 declares, "You will fill me with joy in your presence, with eternal pleasures at your right hand."

I remember this hymn from childhood. "Loved with everlasting love, led by grace that love to know; Spirit, breathing from above, Thou hast taught me it is so."[8]

Knowing God even enriches the joys of this life. He is the one who created these joys and sustains life to make these joys possible. The blessings of life cannot be experienced truly by the one who says in his heart, there is no God.

Spiritual Success

Proverbs 2 is the Bible's primer on true success and its relationship to the fear of the Lord.

> [1]My son, if you accept my words
>   and store up my commands within you,
> [2]turning your ear to wisdom
>   and applying your heart to understanding,
> [3]and if you call out for insight
>   and cry aloud for understanding,
> [4]and if you look for it as for silver
>   and search for it as for hidden treasure,

> ⁵then you will understand the fear of the LORD
>   and find the knowledge of God.
>
> —Proverbs 2:1–5

The person who is an accomplished athlete, or a prosperous businessperson, or a recognized intellectual is thought of as successful. Proverbs 2 defines success as attaining wisdom, understanding, and discretion from God.

> ⁶ For the LORD gives wisdom,
>   and from his mouth come knowledge and understanding.
> ⁷He holds victory in store for the upright,
>   he is a shield to those whose walk is blameless,
> ⁸for he guards the course of the just
>   and protects the way of his faithful ones.
> ⁹Then you will understand what is right and just
>   and fair—every good path.
> ¹⁰For wisdom will enter your heart,
>   and knowledge will be pleasant to your soul.
> ¹¹Discretion will protect you,
>   and understanding will guard you.
>
> —Proverbs 2:6–11

Imagine that you have a thirteen-year-old son. He is brimming with life, anxious to be treated like an adult. He is confronted with powerful temptations. Some temptations come from young men who are arrogant, irreverent, coarse, and bawdy. These young men will attempt to make a disciple of your son. They will pursue him with missionary zeal to turn him from the paths of life into the dark ways of perversity and evil. There is another range of temptations that will come from young women who are alluring and entice your son with flirtations.

How can your son know success in the face of these temptations? It is only through the fear of the Lord.

> ¹²Wisdom will save you from the ways of wicked men,
>   from men whose words are perverse,
> ¹³who leave the straight paths
>   to walk in dark ways,
> ¹⁴who delight in doing wrong
>   and rejoice in the perverseness of evil,
> ¹⁵whose paths are crooked
>   and who are devious in their ways.
> ¹⁶It will save you also from the adulteress,
>   from the wayward wife with her seductive words,

[17]who has left the partner of her youth
   and ignored the covenant she made before God.
[18]For her house leads down to death
   and her paths to the spirits of the dead.
[19]None who go to her return
   or attain the paths of life.

—Proverbs 2:11–19

Wisdom from God is the definition of true success. Good grades, good jobs, even fine artistic skills are empty prizes without godly wisdom. Wisdom will yield success in whatever a young person does.

[20]Thus you will walk in the ways of good men
   and keep to the paths of the righteous.
[21]For the upright will live in the land,
   and the blameless will remain in it.

—Proverbs 2:20–21

The Blessing of Education

LEARNING TO CARE FOR GOD'S WORLD

What is the purpose of education? Psalm 8 answers the question. Mankind has been given dominion over the works of God's hands.

[5]You made him a little lower than the heavenly beings
   and crowned him with glory and honor.
[6]You made him ruler over the works of your hands;
   you put everything under his feet:
[7]all flocks and herds,
   and the beasts of the field,
[8]the birds of the air,
   and the fish of the sea,
   all that swim the paths of the seas.

Education does not exist solely for job training, but to equip mankind for dominion. It is our high privilege to serve God with whatever work we do. We bring to our work the knowledge that it has eternal significance. We are ruling whatever God has given us to do, for our King Jesus.

INCREASING OUR KNOWLEDGE SO WE CAN GLORIFY OUR CREATOR AND SAVIOR

All the departments of human knowledge exist to bring God glory through Jesus Christ. We learn to study, research, organize thoughts and express them cogently so that we can exercise dominion to the glory of God. We develop aesthetic sensitivity so that we can appreciate and promote beauty, develop beautiful public spaces and lovely homes, enjoy wonderful music, and live with dignity that befits creatures made in the image of God. We learn mathematics to quantify things in the creation and predict trends and track satellites so we can serve humanity with the technology that God entrusted to mankind. We develop physical prowess so we have grace of movement, strength, flexibility and stamina that we need to exercise dominion over God's world.

Wisdom redeems and restores education.

Talk with Your Children about Wisdom and Foolishness

Imagine that your young son has been influenced to participate in some act of vandalism or disrespect toward others. You could have a conversation like this.

"You know that what you have done is wrong, don't you?"

"Yeah, I guess."

"We will have to talk about what you have done and how you can make restitution, but I want you to think about this first. There are two kinds of people in the world. Do you remember who they are?" (This is a good time to review your formative instruction.)

"The wise man and the fool."

"You're right; I knew you'd get it. How does the wise man get so wise?"

"The fear of the Lord?"

"You're right, the fear of the Lord. Why is the foolish man so foolish?"

"Because he says in his heart, there is no God."

"Which one do you think showed in your choice today? Why does making a poor choice show that you 'forgot' about God?"

I want him to connect the dots, drawing the connection between his words and actions and the warning of Scripture. Perhaps you find that your children are watching a TV program where people are bawdy, coarse, and obscene. Use Scripture (Eph. 5) to help them discern between the foolish person and the wise person who has nothing to do with the fruitless deeds of darkness but rather reproves them.

We have contrasted wisdom and foolishness. Teach this contrast to your children again and again throughout their formative years. When your children need correction and discipline, the contrast between the wise man and the fool will resonate with them because you have given wise instruction.

CHAPTER 10

Complete in Christ

When our children are confronted with temptation to sin, difficult circumstances, or the sting of the sin of others, we want to show them the beauty of resting in Christ—being complete in him. How can we communicate this concept to an eight or ten-year-old, or even a teenager? Let me suggest a very visual way to give the precious truth of Colossians 2:9–10 to our children. These spiritual concepts have real and tangible implications for our relationships and the circumstances of life. We want to contrast God's provision for us in Christ with life apart from God's provision.

Colossians 2:9–10 tells us about this wonderful work God has done. "In Christ all the fullness of the Deity lives in bodily form, and you have been given fullness in Christ." In Christ we have all we need. Regardless of our temptations and struggles with sin, the difficult circumstances of life, and the sins of others against us, Christ is all we need. That is what it means to be "complete in Christ."

Here is the picture. It should be shown to children one step at a time, with adequate time to "take in" each element. It can be a family worship project for a week or longer, or a personal Bible study with an individual child, especially an older child. Welcome questions that help refine your instruction.

We will examine one step at a time.

Where did relationships come from? Creation? No. They existed before creation. God the Father, God the Son, and God the Holy Spirit have a relationship of love, communication, and purpose that exists

123

in eternity. These elements of relationship are evident in Scripture and are basic to the work of the Trinity.

In John, chapters 14 to 16, Jesus is talking to the disciples. Chapter 17 is Christ's prayer, apparently at the close of this discourse with the disciples. Jesus prays for himself, his disciples, and for all believers. Conversation, cooperation, planning and love are evident everywhere in Christ's prayer to the Father.

Ephesians 1 reflects the same qualities of relationship among the Trinity. The Father chooses, the Son redeems, and the Holy Spirit seals.

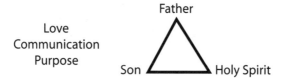

We are made in the image of God. These Trinitarian relationships affect us profoundly. Our relationship with God reflects those same elements—love, communication and purpose (Gen. 1:26, 27).

Adam was made for a relationship of communication, love and purpose with God and correspondingly with Eve and with their offspring. <u>Man needs relationships because he is made in the image of God.</u> Before the Fall relationships were not arduous, but fulfilling. God decided before the Fall that Adam needed a helpmeet. He said, "It is not good for man to be alone." Let's briefly look at the relationships outlined in the creation account.

In Genesis 1:27–2:25 we see that God gave Adam purposeful work to do. He was to subdue the earth, to be fruitful and multiply and to rule over the earth. This direction and instruction demonstrates Adam's dependence on God. Adam was not an automaton. He needed God to describe the proper use and habitation of the garden. Adam was responsible to God, under God's direction and care. He had no life experience. He started out grown-up! Imagine—I'm in a fog sometimes and I at least have good old experience to help interpret daily life.

Man was set apart from all the rest of creation. Genesis 2:7–8, 15 tells us that "The LORD God formed the man from the dust of the ground and breathed into his nostrils the breath of life, and the man became a living being. Now the LORD God had planted a garden in the east, in Eden; and there he put the man he had formed. The LORD God took the man and put him in the Garden of Eden to work it and take care of it."

God created man and immediately spoke to him. Earlier creation did not elicit this response because man alone was designed for relationship with God—with a soul fitted for worship. Man alone was designed for revelation from God. The relationship was purposeful—God gave him work. It was intimate—God breathed into Adam the breath of life and he became a living being. God's love was demonstrated in the provision of the garden as a home with ample supply for all Adam's needs. God extended all the elements of love, communication and purpose to Adam.

God's provision of Eve as a companion for Adam is another expression of his love and poignant care for his image-bearers. God formed Eve from Adam's own body. The intimacy of the creation process spilled out in fellowship, conversation, companionship, direction and instruction. God was their loving authority. Adam and Eve had regular communion with God. They had no fear. There was unbroken communication. What a picture! What a paradise! This was our inheritance before the Fall.

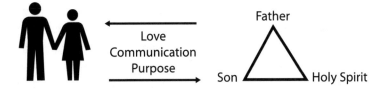

What went wrong? Genesis 3:1–24 summarizes the Fall. The serpent spoke to Eve, "You will be like God . . ." The fruit the serpent offered was desirable. Eve ate and gave it to Adam. He ate. Their eyes were opened. They were filled with shame. Man became like God, knowing good from evil. Man now feared God rather than feeling secure under God's protection.

God came to fellowship with Adam and Eve, but communion was already broken. Adam and Eve were ashamed because of their nakedness and guilty because of their disobedience. Accusations filled their mouths as they desperately tried to cover their disobedience, but the damage was done. Alienation from God stood in the place of that sweet relationship of love, communication and purpose.

How did Adam and Eve change in their relationship to one another? Adam turned on Eve; the one flesh relationship was marred. Deception and suspicion displaced honesty and trust. We hear him passing the buck, blaming Eve, accusing God. "The *woman* you put here with me—she gave me some fruit from the tree, and I ate it."

Adam and Eve were alienated from each other in the same way that they were both alienated from God. All the elements of relationship that were present in perfection before the Fall were lost.

Work took on a burdensome dimension (Gen. 3:16–19). Survival took the place of paradise. The husband/wife relationship was shaped around the necessity to work in a world thwarted by the physical, emotional, relational, and spiritual thorns and thistles of life. Adam, the superintendent and caretaker of paradise, became a common laborer. Work was no longer a joy, but rather arduous labor.

Perfect health and perfect intellect were exchanged for atrophy, deterioration, faulty intellect, depraved minds, decay, death and dying, returning to the dust from which humankind was created.

Eve suffered pain in childbearing. God's proclamation of this fact indicates that this was a change from his former purpose in birth. Try to imagine the joy of bringing new life into the world without the attending discomfort of nine months and the pain of delivery.

Adam and Eve were driven from the Garden of Eden. This would have been the end. But praise God! The relationship was not completely destroyed. While there was total alienation from the just God, there was hope. God promised that Satan would eventually be destroyed.

God cared for Adam and Eve by clothing them—covering their shame. This was a foreshadowing of the work of Christ in shedding his blood as a covering for sin.

God established a covenant: He provided for their survival and redemption. "Through painful toil you will eat." God provided even in the midst of the curse. This was the first instance of common grace. Redemption: "He must not be allowed to reach out his hand and take also from the tree of life and eat, and live forever." In not eating of the tree of life, Adam and Eve were "redeemed" from living eternally in their fallen state. This is mercy.

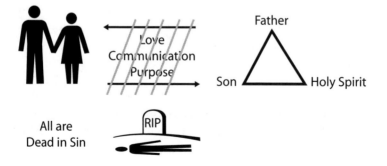

The Fall has serious implications for all of us. When Adam sinned, all mankind sinned (Rom. 5:12–19). Adam was our representative, and we are his descendents. The result of one trespass was condemnation for all men. We are all born enemies of God. We are unable to do anything to change our condition. Romans 3:23, "For all have sinned and fall short of the glory of God."

All people are sinners from conception. There is no one who has a pure heart. All men are God's enemies as a result of Adam's sin (1 Jn. 1:10, "If we claim we have not sinned, we make him out to be a liar." See also 1 Kings 8:46; Ps. 51:5; Rom. 7:14–24.)

We all have a sinful nature. Romans 7:5 says that this sinful nature is in us from the beginning, and that it controls us. Verse 18 says, "I know that nothing good lives in me, that is, in my sinful nature. For I have the desire to do what is good, but I cannot carry it out." Verse 25 says, "I myself in my mind am a slave to God's law, but in the sinful nature a slave to the law of sin."

The problem with man is what he is. What man does is the fruit of what he is. Our hearts, apart from Christ, are wicked. That is why we sin. Luke 6:43–45 says, "No good tree bears bad fruit, nor does a bad tree bear good fruit. Each tree is recognized by its own fruit. People do not pick figs from thornbushes, or grapes from briers. The good man brings good things out of the good stored up in his heart, and the evil man brings evil things out of the evil stored up in his heart. For out of the overflow of his heart his mouth speaks."

All of this leads to God's pronouncement of humankind's condition—we are dead in trespasses and sins. Dead people are unable to help themselves. The only restoration is in the Lord Jesus Christ, who was given to overcome sin and its destruction.

The pitch of the devil to Adam and Eve was this—you don't have to depend on God to know good and evil—you can judge for yourself! That same temptation is with us today.

"God gave them over to shameful lusts" (Rom. 1:26). "They exchanged the truth of God for a lie, and worshiped and served created things rather than the Creator" (Rom. 1:25).

Remember man's history. God created relationships. Man was made for relationship with God. God's relationship with his image bearers, Adam and Eve, involved love, communication and purpose. God met all Adam's needs in that first God/man relationship. Man was designed to need God and to have all his needs satisfied as he worshiped God and lived under God's provision and direction. Revelation was needed before the Fall. God talked with Adam and Eve

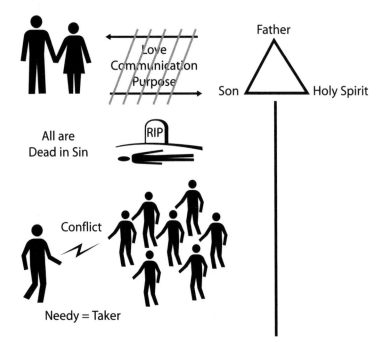

in the cool of the day. He provided direction and fellowship; connection with the Creator. Sin did not bring the need for revelation. Creaturehood did!

When Adam sinned, that relationship was broken. Man became "dead in sin." Relationally, man was left needy and desperate.

All humankind's original needs for love, communication and purpose still exist but now are unsatisfied. These "image-bearing" qualities are essential to man's existence. When people are estranged from God, they reach out with grasping hands to have their needs met horizontally through other people. They expect the people in their lives to do for them what only God can do. It doesn't work! People are met with resistance, hostility and conflict because, apart from Christ, each person has the same agenda . . . to have *my* needs met. People in this condition can only be "takers." This describes and defines how fallen people relate to one another. People without Christ may be nice or even philanthropists, but they are meeting some personal need with their nice or philanthropic relationships.

Romans 1:28–31 describes man's condition. "Furthermore, since they did not think it worthwhile to retain the knowledge of God, he gave them over to a depraved mind, to do what ought not to be done. They have become filled with every kind of wickedness, evil, greed, and depravity. They are full of envy, murder, strife, deceit and

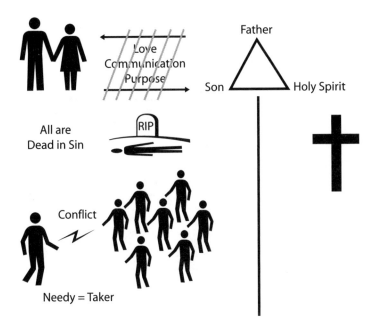

malice. They are gossips, slanderers, God-haters, insolent, arrogant and boastful; they invent ways of doing evil; they disobey their parents; they are senseless, faithless, heartless, ruthless."

God's holiness and justice condemn sin. God's character dictates that he cannot overlook sin. It must be punished by death. Scores

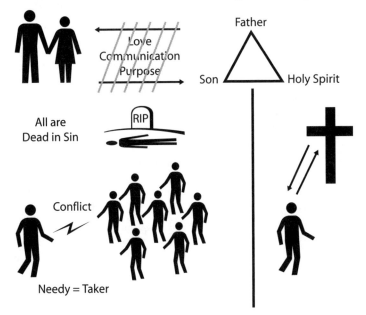

of passages speak of God's anger, wrath and punishment on sin (Ps. 5:4–6; Nahum 1:2–3; Rom. 1:18, 32; 2:5–6, 8–9; 5:9–11; 8:1–4).

God has provided a substitute for us. Jesus Christ, the Son of God, lived a perfect life on our behalf and died to pay the penalty our sin deserves so that his children would not be punished eternally. God discloses his generous grace in passages like 2 Corinthians 5:21, "God made him who had no sin to be sin for us, so that in him we might become the righteousness of God." (See also Isa. 53; Rom. 3:10–31; Heb. 2:14–18; 4:15; 1 Pet. 2:21–24; 1 Jn. 1:7; Mt. 1:21; 1 Cor. 15:3, 55–57.)

We are saved by faith in the sacrifice Christ made for us. There is nothing we can do to save ourselves. It is a gift of grace from God our Father to those who believe in the Lord Jesus Christ.

Through Jesus Christ, there is renewed relationship to God. On the basis of Christ's work, we are reunited with God in the relationship of love, communication and purpose that was severed with Adam's sin. (See 1 Pet. 1:3–9; 2 Cor. 5:17–19; Rom. 6; 8:1–11, 28–39; 1 Jn. 4:7–16; Eph. 4:17–32; 5:1–33, 6:1–24; Col. 3:12–17; Gal. 5:22–26.)

Listen to the contrast between what we were, dead in sin, and what we are now, alive in Christ. <u>We are complete in him</u>.

Praise be to the God and Father of our Lord Jesus Christ! In his great mercy he has given us new birth into a living hope through the

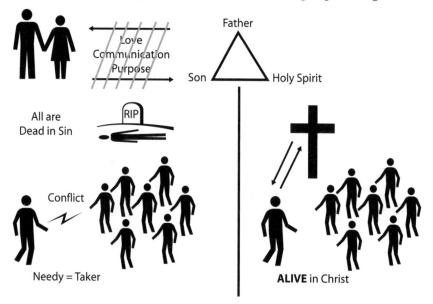

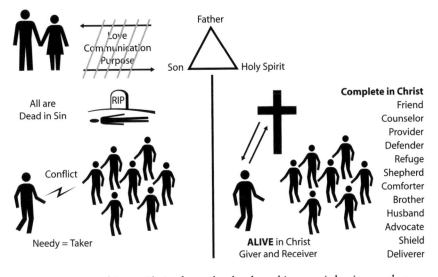

resurrection of Jesus Christ from the dead, and into an inheritance that can never perish, spoil or fade—kept in heaven for you, who through faith are shielded by God's power until the coming of the salvation that is ready to be revealed in the last time. In this you greatly rejoice, though now for a little while you may have had to suffer grief in all kinds of trials. These have come so that your faith—of greater worth than gold, which perishes even though refined by fire—may be proved genuine and may result in praise, glory and honor when Jesus Christ is revealed. Though you have not seen him, you love him; and even though you do not see him now, you believe in him and are filled with an inexpressible and glorious joy, for you are receiving the goal of your faith, the salvation of your souls.

—1 Peter 1:3–9

Praise God for His work. The veil of the temple was rent, the wall of division was torn down! Renewed relationship with God through Christ is the only basis for truly honest human relationships, because our relationship needs are met in Christ.

We can now move toward people in our world with open hands and hearts, *and* receive both good and bad in return. Our needs are no longer met at the expense of others. We are not striving to be okay by virtue of what others do for us, how they treat us, or how they regard us.

Rather than living and responding out of our desperation as fallen people, separated from God, we have access to God through Christ. God has given his Son as the fulfillment of all that we need for love, communication and purpose. We are no longer takers—we are now givers and receivers! The good and bad in our relationships with other people may affect us emotionally (we may experience joy or sorrow), but those relationships do not dictate who we are, how we respond, or how we view ourselves or others.

When we fail to remember God's provision in Christ, God has not neglected us, we have simply forgotten our inheritance for the moment. We are behaving like takers, like spiritual paupers rather than sisters and brothers of Christ—royalty. I sometimes think of it like this. God has welcomed his children, bought by Christ, to live in his courts, with all the spiritual privileges and wealth of his sovereign kingdom. But there are times when we forget our position and we erect little shanties outside the royal courts and take a peek inside from time to time to long after the treasures that are in reality ours.

Note: I have been expansive in describing the visuals because I know that we must have a good grasp of truth ourselves before we can digest it, simplify it, and make it age appropriate for our children.

It is good for us to think of ways to approach all of these spiritual concepts for our children. Whatever progress we make is far better than confusion. They will grow in their understanding of precious truth as we faithfully and creatively teach them.

CHAPTER 11

The Importance of the Church

"Hey, wake up! It's nine o'clock. We have to be at church in half an hour. I have nursery and you're head usher this morning."

"We may as well skip worship service. We will have to leave at eleven thirty to make it to Junior's ball game. It's always so embarrassing to leave early."

"Do you think anyone would notice if I don't make it to small group prayer meeting? I just feel like I have to relax tonight. I need some time to myself."

"Do we have to go to church today, Dad? The whole family is still here after Sis's wedding. By the time we get to the beach this afternoon, we will have missed all the fun."

"I always feel guilty when I miss church. I hate it when people call to ask if I'm okay."

"I'm the only kid in school who'll miss the playoffs tonight because I have to go to church! Man, oh man, Mom! It's just once a year. Give me a break."

Sound familiar? How do you think about "church"? Ask your children, "What is the church and how does the church affect you?" Children often identify a building and the weekly activities as the church, and our attendance to the facility and its programs as our involvement. Certainly, the building and its activities are a part of the tangible expression of *what* the church is. But that doesn't even scratch the surface of God's grand vision and purpose for the church. Our children need this picture to energize their faithfulness to this essential means of grace in their lives. Church life is an accurate and biblical cultural model for your family. How can we effectively teach them how important it is?

God has designed everything in the creation to declare his story! The church is rich with pictures that teach us who God is, what he has done and our place in it all. Our formative instruction will dramatically affect our children's responses to this activity.

How do I prepare for church?

Allow the pictures that follow to awaken you and your children for the Lord's Day, or better yet, to prepare your hearts on Saturday for the Lord's Day! Answer your children's questions about your physical church home with spiritual truth and insight, which will give the physical church fresh importance in your family life and personal lives.

The Church Is God's Family

God designed people to live in community—both physical and spiritual. We are born into a physical family. The family is essential to the growth and development of each of its members. God created the family in such a way that the family facilitates our understanding of the church. God extended the tactile experience of family to unfold for us the nature of the church—the family of God. Our families are a precious representation of the family of God, with worship, training, leadership, submission, roles, schedule, laws, accountability, humility, unity, diversity, common goals, love, thanksgiving, praise, nurture, protection, refuge, healing, witness, hospitality, compassion, stewardship, consideration, forgiveness, servanthood, bearing one another's burdens, acceptance, encouragement, communion, companionship, admonition, rebuke, restoration, repentance, reconciliation, prayer and fellowship, to name just a few. These qualities are essential to a healthy, happy family. The same qualities make the church an essential community for our children and us. Our spiritual health and well-being depends on God's provision of a spiritual community just as our children's overall well-being depends on the family we provide for them. God delivers children into the family at birth as a picture of his purpose to "deliver" his children into the spiritual family, the church, by new birth. Children who experience the beautiful analogy of the family from their earliest remembrances have ring-side seats to God's redemptive pageant played out in the church.

the need for a spiritual comm.

The family of God gets the reputation we live out in our homes. Children are prepared for their experience of the church family by their experience in our own families. That's why God uses familial terms to describe himself as a Father, Christ as the Son, us as his sons and daughters, Christ as our brother, the church as Christ's bride, and fellow Christians as sisters and brothers. Our experiences of those sensory family relationships give meaning to spiritual relationships. We must train our children to think of the church as their spiritual family.

church is our spiritual family

Church isn't the place where you are obligated to go, but the place you want to be, just as you want to be with your family. Your spiritual responsibilities aren't what you have to do, but what you love to do, out of the same kind of love and commitment you feel for your family. Psalm 122:1 is our song as we prepare for the Lord's Day, "I rejoiced with those who said to me, 'Let us go to the house of the LORD.'"

Use all the dynamics of family life to paint this picture. Speak of your "sisters and brothers" with true endearment and genuine appreciation for their ministries to you. Extol the family qualities listed above aloud to your family as you experience them. The old adage is true: "Truth is better caught than taught."

"Sally called to ask how I was feeling and prayed for me over the phone. What an encouragement she is."

"John is letting us use his car while ours is being repaired. He is living out God's purpose for brothers in Christ to 'bear one another's burdens.' We can be thankful!"

"I know you were hurt by Cindy's insensitive remark after Sunday school, Honey, but Paul reminded the Colossian Christians in Colossians 3:12–13, "Therefore, as God's chosen people, holy and dearly loved, clothe yourselves with compassion, kindness, humility, gentleness and patience. Bear with each other and forgive whatever grievances you may have against one another. Forgive as the Lord forgave you. And over all these virtues put on love, which binds them all together in perfect unity."

Your children themselves are a picture of God's children. Dependence and trust mark a child's relationship with a parent. Earthly parents work tirelessly to provide safety, security, nurture, understanding, shelter, love, protection, guidance and instruction, discipline, chastisement, restoration, physical comfort, health, and care in sickness—everything needed for their children's well-being. God does the same for his children. We have some sense, even in a fallen world where earthly fathers fall short of perfection, of the Father's love and care because he chose to identify us as his children. People whose fathers were abusive exclaim when they come to faith in Christ, "I never understood what it meant that God is our Father before knowing his love and care." What a beautiful thought. In this twisted world, God's love sets the record straight. If our human experience does not give a glimpse of his awesome character, then a glimpse of him reshapes our human experience!

Adoption   Human adoption is another picture of God making us part of the family of God. God uses even the painful experience of the orphan in a broken world to paint glorious pictures of his provision for his children in Christ. Lonely, lost, empty, forgotten children are chosen by caring, capable parents, to live in the beauty of family—to have companionship, to belong, to have the full experience of meaningful and purposeful relationships with others. Being chosen means everything to the orphan. It was not the luck of the draw. These human saviors found a particular orphan to touch their hearts—the one they longed to lavish with love, protection, nurture, direction and provision.

"For he **chose** us in him before the creation of the world to be holy and blameless in his sight. In love he predestined us to be **adopted** as his sons through Jesus Christ, in accordance with his pleasure and will" (Eph. 1:4–5; emphasis mine).

"I will call them 'my people' who are not my people; and I will call her 'my loved one' who is not my loved one" (Rom. 9:25).

The Church Is an Extension of Our Family

God designed the means of safely delivering our children gradually from the primary community of the family to a broader family that supports the worldview of the family. That is the church. Family life and church life are intended to run parallel over our child's developmental years. This will encourage their movement from our family community to the church community, where God the Father, Christ the brother, and earthly sisters and brothers in Christ become their personal experience.

Think of the elements of family life listed earlier and reflect on life in the body of Christ. In a culture where everything regarding the church and God is suspect, we must understand and practice biblical church life that gives meaning, purpose, dignity and divine intention to human life. God has designed the church community to safely extend all the ministries of the family for the nurture and development of our children and us. We should discuss these thoughts with our children. The church is an essential element of the culture we provide for our children.

The Church Supports Our Christian Worldview

Christian parents face a grave challenge in today's culture. The church of Christ is the only place where our standards are believed and applied. <u>The church provides support structures for our worldview and teaches values that parallel the values of our homes.</u>

supports what we teach at home.

① *Family worship,* where God is joyfully and reverently honored with thanksgiving, prayer, singing, Bible reading and praise, is expanded in corporate worship. That gives weight and significance to your daily routine. It's not just your little family who does this daily ritual—<u>there are others, old and young, who worship God as you do.</u>

Family worship is daily practice for corporate worship. Thanksgiving and singing God's praises on the Lord's Day is not arduous if it is our joyful daily routine. But worship comes haltingly and awkwardly from unpracticed hearts and lips. Participation in family worship also prepares the heart and mouth for corporate prayer and testimony, from the father to the youngest children.

② *Training* is defined as repeated action for the sake of obtaining a competency or ability. All of our training at home, all of our children's efforts to achieve our standards or those they have marked out for themselves, have these objectives. Our church community, Sunday school teachers, youth leaders, worship leaders and preachers have the same calling to the same spiritual goals.

<u>Prayer is just such a training process.</u> In our homes, we pray as a first resort in all of the joys and trials of life. We thank God for his provision, whether it comes from his hand as a result of our work or God surprises us with provision from his vast storehouses (we receive finances for a needed car that no one knew about). We recognize that we are finite in the face of trials and that our infinite heavenly Father can be trusted with our dilemma, so we go to him before creating a solution to our needs. This is not how the world operates. Sadly, much of the church is no better. How often do Christians say, "Well, I guess all we can do is pray!"

The worldly person takes full credit for providing their daily bread and even talks about how lucky they are when things just "fall into their lap." When troubles come, they formulate plans and manipulate finances and people to hedge their bets.

For our families, the training process of "taking it to the Lord in prayer" is an ongoing demonstration that we believe God answers prayer (Mk. 11:24), that he is able to do abundantly more than we can ask or imagine (Eph. 3:20), that his purposes toward us are good (Rom. 8:28), and that rest and peace for our souls will be found in entrusting our deepest needs to God (Phil. 4:6). The church loves to pray for all the same reasons. The church encourages and extends our training.

③ *God's Word* is our only rule for faith and practice. The church underscores this belief in its preaching and teaching for all age groups.

Biblical laws and standards sound oppressive and restrictive in our lawless, arrogant twenty-first century culture. But the psalmists rhapsodize about the law of God as sweet, precious, life-giving, wise, pure, enlightening, liberating and good. In our homes, we follow the absolutes and principles of Scripture and apply them to the "stuff" of family life. The church supports our love of the law of God as satisfying and necessary for an edifying and productive life.

④ *Loving authority* in our homes is not only supported by the church, but extended in the authority structures of the church. Hierarchy is established by God and taught in Scripture as the pattern for all of life. Parental roles are primary in the life of the home and church as fathers and mothers lead, love, and nurture their families, and as children grow up in the fear and admonition of the Lord under the loving rule of parents.

The church teaches hierarchy, accountability to God, and accountability to the authorities he has established in the home, church and government. Accountability is a lost notion in our individualistic culture. It's every man for himself! Not so in the Christian family. The church community expects that we will fulfill our roles joyfully knowing that accountability to authority is honorable and beneficial to everyone. Accountability creates a refuge from the deceitfulness and foolishness of our own hearts. Relationships in the church also build mutual accountability, which protects us from our own sin and foolishness.

⑤ *Submission* is a beautiful concept that bears the fruit of a biblical sense of well-being, protection, fulfillment, security and proportion to all who grasp God's order in the cosmos. Our secular culture distorts submission to mean servility, disgrace, stupidity, disrespect and degradation. The church practices the appropriateness and dignity of submission as the design of God in all of its offices and functions.

The Scriptures are thorough. They balance teaching about submission in every area of life with the safety valves of appeal to authority, and even illustrations of obedience to God as the higher authority over unworthy earthly authorities.

Roles define the practice of submission in your home. The world believes that equality and submission are enemies. They are not enemies. Galatians 3:28 teaches us that all of humankind stands equal before God. We do not submit to authority because we are inferior in any way. Neither do we rule in any sphere of life because we are superior. But God has created roles that are consistent with the hierarchy he lovingly dictated for his image-bearers. The church encourages God's designated roles and further defines authority and submission in its offices and in its life as a body. Church life further supports submission as church members lovingly submit to each other for the good of the church as a whole.

The church provides a context for our children to have relationships with other adults who love them and care about them and their future, and who also share our values and goals. These adults model biblical manhood and womanhood for our children in a culture where gender specific roles are melting away.

Caring relationships within the community of faith are a way of life for believers. We strive for our homes to practice gracious and welcoming hospitality to all people. We show compassion to people suffering all kinds of trials. We are watchful for others who need help with their burdens. We give our time, energy, resources and abilities in service to others. We strive to develop servants' hearts in our children.

You see the wisdom and righteousness in striving for unity in your family and in all the communities in which you live and work. You forgive and love even when wronged and rejected. You are quick to hold hands with others who have common goals rather than isolating yourself. You rejoice in diversity of personality, abilities and roles as God's perfect design. Humility in relationship to God and in relationship to others is your family posture.

The church is a safe context for identifying true diversity, for children to practice life skills, for getting sea legs before sailing on life's seas. When the world beckons to our children, they will find it hard to deny and forsake a whole community who loves and accepts them. However, be careful that you do not blame the church when your children reject it. There are also reasons in their own hearts that lead them away.

God's Word designates right and wrong, form and freedom, truth and falsehood. Christian liberty can be enjoyed and celebrated in the church without the pollution of humanism before children are confronted with the fraudulent freedoms assumed by worldly-minded peers.

These activities are the context, outside of your home, to practice your role as "light and salt."

The Church Teaches and Supports These Family Activities

Education is a huge consideration for the Christian family. The Scriptures demonstrate God's purpose that parents be the primary teachers in the lives of their children. That is true whether or not parents choose home schooling, Christian school, or public school.

parents are the 1ˢᵗ teachers

This is not the world's perspective. Secular humanism has wrestled the primary role of training and development from parents. Parents have become increasingly preoccupied with themselves—pursuing work, entertainment, prosperity, or simply surviving.

The church supports Christian education in the home, church and Christian school as a primary means of instilling Christian ethics, morality and worldview in the minds and hearts of our children. The church recognizes parents as God's primary agents of nurture, instruction, motivation and discipline for children.

Schedule, entertainment, pastimes and free time are all really a discussion of priorities. Your family life is shaped around the activities you believe are most desirable to accomplish your goals to be a healthy family physically, emotionally and spiritually. Poor stewardship of time, energy and financial resources rob you of all the spiritual blessings God promises to those who are in pursuit of the kingdom of heaven.

priorities

what do I desire most?

In addition to worship, a primary calling for the church is to strive, by Christ's grace and the Spirit's work, toward physical, emotional and spiritual health in preparation for that day when we will be presented as a spotless bride to Christ.

Individual relationships in this world are shaped by our most basic beliefs. Qualities in relationships are dramatically different for the believer and unbeliever. Christian homes emulate consideration, forgiveness, acceptance, encouragement, communion, companionship, self-sacrificing love, admonition, rebuke, restoration, repentance, reconciliation, fellowship, nurture, loyalty, refuge, healing, and accountability. These are either unfamiliar, or mean something very different in the secular community.

Love is a good illustration. The Christian formula for love is, "Better love has no man than this, to lay down his life for his brother." The secular mind believes that everyone has to do his part for love to be reasonable. Therefore, "I'll give fifty percent if you will. If you don't hold up your end of the bargain, I'm out of here!"

Forgiveness follows the same argument. "If you ask forgiveness and acknowledge what you've done to my satisfaction, I'll accept your apology. But I maintain the right to withhold friendship from you until I believe you have paid sufficiently."

The Church Is Our Spiritual Shelter

The sweetest aspect of family life is the shelter it provides in a fallen and callous world. Family members love and support one another when the world doesn't know or care about our struggles or losses. There is acceptance and forgiveness for failures. A family member gives humble warning and even loving admonishment when physical or spiritual danger threatens his loved one. Feasting and provision can always be found at home. There is always enough love, always enough kindness, always enough patience to go around. The family circle gives courage and determination to go back to the marketplace of life. God designed the nuclear family to be a refuge to facilitate our understanding of the church.

[handwritten margin note: then our families must actually do this. Do we do it well?]

God provides the same shelter for his family, the church. Even the loss of family illustrates his fatherly care—both physically and spiritually. The Old Testament displays God's physical care of the fatherless and widow in the absence of natural family. "A father to the fatherless, a defender of widows. . . . God sets the lonely in families" (Ps. 68:5–6). God covenants with his people, "I will be a Father to you and you will be my sons and daughters" (2 Cor. 6:18).

Mutual fellowship, communion, encouragement, admonition and feasting serve the body of Christ just as those qualities make the family strong. Let me quote an excerpt from an essay by Mr. Aaron Tripp, *The Glorious War*, regarding the Sabbath day shelter of the church.

Just as we must stop our outdoor work each night, not because we have the sense to, but because we are forced inside by the darkness, so each seventh day, since God rested on that day from the work of creating he had done, we take our rest. On that day it is as though the battle were done. We stop, for a moment, from the unending struggle with our foe. We live, for a day, as though we were already victorious. Like victorious warriors returning from battle, we crowd into the hall of our king, we sit down to the feast he has prepared for us, and we look forward to the day when the battle will done, when the final enemy will fall, when the rule of our king will be imposed on the whole created order, when Everlasting Night will be cast down forever, and Dread Chaos abolished. On that day the enemies of order will fall and never rise again.

So in we come, like conquerors, and we join one another at the table, and rejoice in our victorious king, and take our rest. For a brief time we are not surrounded by enemies on all sides; the whole world does not strive against us, or seek to destroy our resolve. We are surrounded by our comrades, our brothers in arms, heroes in the battle. We exult to be together with such heroes, we know what dreadful foes they have faced, how sorely they were pressed, how they maintained their purposes, how they strove, how they trusted the puissance of their king in the darkest hours, how they overcame the enemy, how they strove for the glory of their lord, how they sought to conform the world to a pattern which would honor him.

They know, likewise, what terrors we have known in battle, how we have sorrowed, how we have grown weak. They have striven beside us against our enemy. When our hearts failed us they turned our eyes to the majestic standard of our savior. So together we come, brothers in arms, not now striving, but fellowshipping, and encouraging, and glorying together in our king.

On the first day of the week we return to the war. We are renewed, our armor is repaired, it is even made stronger. Our hearts, which might otherwise despair of so long a struggle, are made strong. Our wounds are bound up and healed. Out we go to war, for the glory of our King, and we are not weary, we do not lose heart, we give no ground to the enemy; we advance; we look forward to the coming Sabbath, and we long for our eternal rest.

The Church Explains the Trials of Life for the Believer

In Ephesians 5:22–33, Paul uses marriage to identify the church as Christ's bride. Verses 25 through 27 tell us that Christ is purifying his bride, making her ready for eternity with the bridegroom. She will be radiant, without stain or wrinkle or any other blemish.

You and I and our children are unfit to be such a bride. Praise God, Christ's perfect life and death on the cross secured the church's betrothal, because there is justification for all who repent and believe. Ephesians 5 identifies sanctification. Christ's purpose in the trials of life is to make us radiant. He is like a refiner's fire (Mal. 3:2–4). We are like gold and silver that is polluted by the soil from which it was dug. The artisan applies scorching heat and blasting cold to make a thing of beauty. The struggles and trials of this life are to make us beautiful for eternity. This is expressed beautifully in a poem by Walter Wangerin, Jr., "Earth, Fire, Water, Air" with the lines,

> Drive fire through all my being
> And let no vein not know the caustic shot of cleansing.[9]

The church is the community of Christ's redeemed people from all times and places, from the creation of the Garden of Eden until Christ comes again in power and glory. Our local assemblies are individual expressions of the universal church. When your children complain that the Christian life seems hard by comparison with the carefree world, remind them that a great day is coming, when this carefree world will be without a lover, alone and cast out into eternal darkness, without hope of deliverance. All of the dainty charms and alluring pleasures of this world will be unmasked. Those who have endured the purifying fires of trials will have robes fit for a beloved bride awaiting the Savior-bridegroom. I want to be a known and participating member of the bride—the church!

The Church Has Implications for Your Family

Church is usually a family priority for believers. That is good and appropriate. But parents shape how their children think about church life. Magnify the beauty of the corporate life of your church. It is an essential element of Christian culture. If attendance to church and its activities are a burdensome obligation that competes with other more desirable pastimes, children will live for the day they can opt out of attendance. All of the optional activities of life, learning skills, sports, employment, entertainment and even education must be scheduled around the church. Otherwise, it will be one among many of the life options for your children—not the deciding factor in prioritizing life.

We need to show them its more!

If it is nothing more than a social organization, children will take it or leave it based on their interest in the social opportunities it offers. How "cool" the youth director is or how "hip" the kids are at church will determine your child's interest. If you are critical and offended by the church family, they will be too, but they will take it a step further and leave.

If the worship and praise of God warm your heart and you find relationships with God's people satisfying and refreshing, and you love nothing more than to use your energy, time, resources and creativity to benefit the body of Christ—then your children will have a perspective from which to admire and appreciate God's family. You cannot secure their membership in this family through yours, but your recruitment skills will be a primary tool in the Spirit's work in their heart.

PART THREE

Application of Formative Instruction

CHAPTER 12

Getting from Behavior to the Heart

In chapter five we saw the biblical teaching that all behavior is driven by the heart. Remember the story in that chapter of the two children arguing over the same toy? Asking the question "who had it first?" fails to address the heart issues. Recall Jesus' words in Mark 7:21–23, "For from within, out of men's hearts, come evil thoughts, sexual immorality, theft, murder, adultery, greed, malice, deceit, lewdness, envy, slander, arrogance and folly. All these evils come from inside and make a man 'unclean.'"

The Danger of Missing the Heart

We can fail to address the heart in correction and discipline. We are tempted to focus on the behavior that requires correction, rather than the heart issues that are the source of bad behavior. When the focus is limited to changed behavior, our response will sound like this:

"Share the toy."

"Leave your sister alone."

"Stop doing that."

We may even succumb to the temptation to manipulate our children's behavior, "It is so sad to see children who have so many nice toys fighting like this. You should both be ashamed; I know I am ashamed of you."

"If you can't play without fighting I'm going to send you to your rooms."

[handwritten margin note: change beh or the heart]

147

Some parents develop very elaborate schemes of manipulation. One dad told me that he had tried to use a "shut up" jar at his home.

"What's a 'shut up jar'?"

"I got so tired of hearing my children say shut up. I told them whenever they say shut up, they must put a dollar in the jar."

"What happened?"

"In two weeks we had one hundred dollars!"

"A hundred dollars, that's a lot of money."

"Yeah, I know, my wife and I were putting some money in too."

"What happened then?"

> It is good and appropriate for a parent to praise what is praiseworthy in their children and to do so sincerely. It is good at times to reward a job well done. I am only questioning praise or rewards as tools of manipulation.

"A couple of weeks passed and no one was saying shut up. So I figured we had learned our lesson. A Friday night came along and I took the family out for pizza, a movie and ice cream. We blew most of the one hundred dollars."

"What happened then?"

"You wouldn't believe it; within two days they were saying shut up again."

Think about this scenario with me. What was going on with these children? Had they experienced heart change? No, all that had changed with these children was their behavior. Once the external force manipulating their behavior was removed (a one dollar fine for saying shut up), their behavior reverted back to the most natural expression of their hearts. This dad had been successful at controlling behavior for the moment, but the children had not been moved an inch in the direction of loving God and others.

There is an almost infinite variety of ways that we can manipulate the behavior of our children. We can bribe them, threaten them, shame them, heap guilt on them, make promises to them, negotiate with them, praise them, or reward them, all in an effort to secure the behavioral outcomes we desire. Sometimes people feel more justified if they are using positive incentives rather than negative disincentives. Whether we use "a carrot or a stick," it is all behaviorism.

Behaviorism Evaluated

Many parents have said to me, "I use a little behaviorism; don't knock it, it works." So what is wrong with behaviorism?

Behaviorism Does Not Address the Real Need of Our Children

To use the words of Jesus, "Out of the overflow of his heart his mouth speaks" (Lk. 6:45). Addressing the behavior without speaking to the heart bypasses the profound needs of the heart. It is like trying to solve the problem of weeds in the yard by using a lawn mower. You might succeed at mowing down the weeds, but you will be dismayed with how quickly they grow back.

Behaviorism Provides Our Children with a False Basis for Ethics

The basis for ethical choices in behaviorism is pragmatic. Parents want a certain outcome of behavior, and children learn to choose their behavior based on punishment or reward. When God responds to his children's behavior, he too is concerned about their actions. But more than that, God is concerned with the heart motives of his children.

In a biblical vision, the basis for ethical decisions is the being, existence and glory of God. Biblical ethics reasons, "There is a God who has made me and all things. He tells me what to do for my good and his glory." As we deal with the external behavior of our children, we also need to teach them to make decisions based on things deeper than anticipated punishment or reward. The fact that there is a God in heaven who has revealed his will to mankind forms the basis for decision-making.

[handwritten margin note: what is my basis for decisions?]

Behaviorism Trains the Heart in Wrong Paths

There is such a close connection between the heart and behavior that whatever is used to constrain the behavior trains the hearts of our children. When a child is manipulated through shame, he learns to respond to shame. When guilt is used as a motive, he may grow to be a guilt-laden adult. If pride is the motivation, he may develop into a person whose concern is the fear of man or the desire to have the approval of people. And frequently homes where anger was used to beat family members into submission, produce angry adults.

Behaviorism Obscures the Message of the Gospel

The gospel will never be central in discipline, correction and motivation when behavior is manipulated. The parent who resorts to

Often I have been asked by the moms of toddlers, "How can I help my two-year-old understand heart issues?" My answer is, "You can't."

A two-year-old is not self-conscious about motivations. He does not have the maturity to think introspectively, or the insight and vocabulary to identify motives. This will have to wait until a child has developed the understanding and vocabulary to think about the subtle attitudes of the heart.

Parents of preschoolers can begin to introduce attitudes of heart by speaking of selfishness, anger, love, hatred and so forth. As you use these terms your child will grow in his perception of their meaning.

Preschool is a time when parents are teaching God's law by making appropriate interventions, such as kindly correcting a child who has taken a toy from another child by saying, "Honey, you must give that back to brother. He was playing with it and it is not right for you to take it from him; that is not loving your brother."

shame, guilt, threats or bribes is not placing their hope of change in the gospel.

Behaviorism Shows the Parent's Idols

There are many reasons parents use behaviorism to control their children. Perhaps we are motivated by pride; our children are our calling card after all. Maybe it is simply a matter of ease. Worse yet we are sometimes driven to control others. Maybe we are driven by the fear of man: We worry about what others will think of us if we seem ineffective with our children.

Many idols of the heart will pollute our interventions with our children. These idols will not motivate us to act for the well-being of our child, but for our own reputations. Thus, our child's good is not the driving force in our correction and discipline, but rather our personal sense of well-being. Our behavior in discipline is motivated by *our* hearts. This does not show the depth of concern for our children's spiritual well-being.

Connecting Heart Attitudes with Behavior

Think about ungodly heart attitudes that we sometimes see in our children. For example, we see times when they are motivated by the desire for revenge. Our children defend themselves with words such as, "That child hit me first." When a child makes that defense, there is an attitude of heart that has motivated behavior—the desire for revenge.

We must teach them to entrust themselves to God. This is what Jesus did when he was persecuted, mocked and even beaten. He entrusted himself to the One who judges justly (1 Pet. 2:23). Instead of responding to his tormentors with retaliation, he went to his Father with trust.

Our children may be motivated by the fear of man. Teens may ignore younger siblings to look cool to school friends. They may say and do what pleases the crowd rather than what would honor God. Fear of man may even result in a child showing greater loyalty to friends than to siblings or parents.

We are tempted to scold or even threaten our children for unkindness. But we know that scolding won't change attitudes of heart.

Pride is often at the heart of conflict children have in the home. Your son lost the Monopoly game. He is upset. He knows it was only a game and not even Boardwalk or Park Place has any real value. He may be upset due to wounded pride (especially if the winner is younger or a girl).

> In placing the focus on heart issues rather than behavior, we are not suggesting that it is always wrong to correct behavior. We must correct behavior in many situations. If your son is cruelly taunting his sister, you cannot wait for heart change. You must censure wrong behavior. However, even when he has stopped what he was doing, you must realize that your job is not over. You will need to help him understand the ways his words reflect a heart that has strayed from God's ways.

Help him understand the pride that motivates his response. You have an opportunity to speak with him about humility. Humility comes before honor.

A child's crass love of self is often transparent. Loving self comes naturally. Teach your children to love others. Christ is the premiere example of one who loved others. He not only models love, he can empower them to love.

Every Christian couple wants their children to be dazzled by God, to behold his splendor and respond with reverential awe. The fear of the Lord is the impetus to these responses from your children.

In chapter five we listed couplets of godly and ungodly attitudes of heart. It would be profitable to review and discuss them with your children. These issues of motivation underlie the things children say and do.

Times of correction are times to build on the foundation we have laid in formative instruction. Help your children to see the connection between behavior that is wrong and heart attitudes that led to that behavior.

The Slippery Slope of Parental Hypocrisy

Manipulating behavior will end up hypocritically distancing me from my children. I will find myself saying things like this, "I can't believe that you are so selfish. Your little brother is going to take a nap in five minutes. Would it kill you to let him play with your Tonka truck for five minutes?"

I would submit that this is hypocrisy toward my son. Who is better acquainted with the ways that selfishness works in the human heart than I? If the truth were told, I could write the book on selfishness.

Do you see what I have done? I have hypocritically distanced myself from my son. I am shaming him for the same crass selfishness that I find in myself. I am focused on behavior and missing the heart. When I act so hypocritically, there will be no gospel, no hope and no grace in my correction.

Getting to the Heart of Behavior

Ask good questions to help your children understand their attitudes of heart.

Think, for example, of the young man who has humiliated his younger brother in the presence of his older friends. You must correct his rude and hurtful behavior, but the wise parent will also help him understand what motivated him. You might have a conversation like this:

"Do you think your brother was embarrassed by the ways you spoke to him?"

"Yeah, I guess."

"Why do you think he felt so hurt?"

"I guess he thought I was making fun of him."

"I think you're right, he did. This is a hard question, but what do you think was going on in your heart when you made fun of him? I know you love your brother, but why do you think you made him feel so bad?"

"I don't know."

"I'll accept that. I don't know either, but let me help you think it through. Are you willing to work on this with me?"

"Yeah, I guess."

"Well, it seems like there are several possibilities. It could be pride, or perhaps love of self, or maybe the fear of man (he is an embarrassment to you), or maybe you just desire the approval of your friends so much that you wanted to look cool to them. What do you think?"

Notes

Let's make some notes on this conversation. Note first that I am not making accusations. I am only trying to get my son to analyze what happened. Secondly, I am not making assessments. I am not telling him what his motives are. I cannot know his heart, and while I might have my suspicions, I am not able to declare his motives. Thirdly, all I want to accomplish at this moment is to encourage self-assessment. I am

> I am not suggesting that every time your child needs correction you will drag him through this kind of process. That would exhaust both him and you. There may be situations in which you correct the behavior and leave it at that. Observe your child's typical responses and look for opportunities to speak to him in depth regarding attitudes of heart.

facilitating the conversation. I am using my greater awareness of heart issues to expand his understanding of the things that motivate his behavior.

It is not necessary for me to close the deal in this conversation. If he begins to get testy, if I begin to get upset, I can always end the discussion. I may say, "You know what, I just wanted you to be able to get a shot at identifying your motives. Believe me, I know how hard that is to do. Let me pray with you and we can talk about this another time. I love you."

Keeping the Gospel Central

I illustrated earlier the hypocrisy of shaming our children. That, of course, is where I will always end up when I am trying to manipulate behavior. If, however, I deal with the heart, I will no longer be hypocritically distanced from my son. I can stand in solidarity with him and his struggles with selfishness. I can put my arm around him and say, "I understand what you are experiencing. I understand selfishness. Dad has his own struggles with being selfish."

I am not excusing selfishness as okay since I am selfish too. Rather, I am simply identifying with this common struggle with sin. Not only do I understand the struggle, I know where I must go with my struggles with selfishness. I must take these struggles to Jesus Christ where I can find forgiveness and grace to help in my time of need.

Jesus Christ has experienced the same kind of temptations that I experience (Heb. 4:14–16). Though he never failed, I often fail in these temptations and must continually seek grace and strength from Jesus Christ. He is able to forgive and to cleanse me (1 Jn. 1:9). He is full of mercy for past failure and grace for present and future need.

As I help my children with this issue of selfishness, I am like a seasoned veteran on the battlefield. I have been in the battle for a longer time. I have a better knowledge of how to do this spiritual warfare. My young children may just be beginning this battle with sin. I can get into the trenches with them and show them where there is hope and strength for this battle.

CHAPTER 13

Corrective Discipline—
Applying the Sowing and Reaping
Principle of Scripture

A quick review is in order. Remember, during times of corrective discipline we must appeal to formative instruction that helps children to understand all the issues of life from the perspective of God's reve- *worldview* lation, the Bible. Sowing and reaping is a profound life lesson that teaches children to think about the consequences and implications of the things they say and do.

In Galatians 6:7–8 sowing and reaping is defined both positively and negatively, "Do not be deceived: God cannot be mocked. A man reaps what he sows. The one who sows to please his sinful nature, from that nature will reap destruction; the one who sows to please the Spirit, from the Spirit will reap eternal life."

It is as important for us to encourage "sowing to the Spirit" as it is to warn against "sowing to the sinful nature." Our formative instruction should abound with the good purposes God the Father had for man before the Fall and his marvelous provision for man after the Fall, through the person and work of his Son, Jesus Christ. The sober reality of his judgment, wrath and intolerance with sin should drive people to the foot of the cross because they are mindful of his amazing grace.

The degree to which the Scriptures are used as a threat in our instruction of children is alarming. This is a distorted portrayal of God and it sends our children scattering before his Law. A powerful judge, without mercy, makes the law harsh and unsparing, rather than protecting and life-giving.

Corrective Discipline

During instances of corrective discipline we appeal to formative instruction to help children understand the issues of life—how sin has affected all of life and the great purposes of God in providing redemption and hope in their time of need. Corrective discipline is the sowing and reaping principle of Scripture at work.

Corrective discipline is a rescue mission, designed to direct straying or unbelieving children back inside the circle of blessing where they honor and obey parents (Eph. 6:1–2). This includes obedience to authorities designated by parents.

It is a beautiful picture. The parent is not standing over the child wielding the law. Rather the parent is instead coming alongside the child as a fellow creature who has tasted the waters of life and can attest to its life-giving qualities (Ps. 34). Christ modeled such a relationship for us. He was made like his brothers in every way so that he may be a merciful and faithful high priest in service to God (Heb. 2:17–18). Philippians 2:1–11 describes his descent into human likeness so that we may be reconciled to God. Hebrews 4:14–16 describes his identification with us for the sake of our victory over sin. He stood beside us, embraced us and showed us the way to God. That is God's purpose in correction and discipline. God is not trying to catch us, or expose us or make us pay. His goal is to make us like Christ. Our discipline and correction should reflect the holy purpose God has for us. It should reflect the same humility, patience, long-suffering and hope that our Savior shows to us.

modeling

Parents often complain, how can I ever accomplish all that you're recommending? Let it be an encouragement to you to know that formative instruction saves the day. All the formal and informal opportunities to teach children the Scriptures prepare the way for correction and discipline. Children will understand your correction and discipline because they have learned from your formative instruction.

The Reaping Process

There are important steps to teaching the reaping process that cannot be ignored if we are going to be biblical rather than behavioristic. *address* These steps use biblical consequences to address the heart. Let me *the heart* illustrate. Your son Billy is complaining. He doesn't like what you made for breakfast. Worse—you didn't wash his favorite shirt for school today. He's angry with his sister because she "touched" his stuff, so he dumped her purse out on the floor and broke her mirror. Billy has already transgressed the circle of Ephesians 6:1–3.

Let's take Billy through the reaping process. How can we use God's model for correction and restoration to address Billy's behavior? And where do consequences fit in?

Note: There is a danger in scripting conversation with Billy. This is only a suggestive conversation. There are many ways to actually say the things that need saying. There are also many variables that may alter the conversation, such as Billy's age, personality, or whether he has professed faith in Christ. Also his own response to what has happened can be anywhere on the continuum from hardheartedness to sorrow over his sin. One part of your conversation will dictate how to proceed with other aspects of your talk with him. The order of the process is not as important as your spirit and goal to bring the gospel to your child. Please don't allow some troubling aspect of the actual conversation to obscure the overall objective.

Ask questions to draw your child out. Identify the situation. "What did you do?"

"Billy, let's think about what has happened. I am concerned about you. We have noticed lately that you struggle with complaining and anger. Do you know what I mean?"

Response

The answer is yes or no. If yes, go on. If no, illustrate. Get acknowledgment, even if it is only a nod. Always dialogue—never monologue. Ask what your child was thinking and feeling that prompted the behavior. What fears, desires, hopes and lusts were in his heart? Of course, the child's age will dictate the nature of the questions.

If he says, I dunno, give multiple choices and let him choose. If he won't acknowledge his sinful behavior, don't accuse. Even if he was "caught in the act," accusations are destructive. If his guilt is certain, come alongside him and tell him kindly but firmly that the "jig is up"—you know of his guilt. Then urge him to "come clean." He is much more likely to confess if your manner is kind than if it is accusing and authoritarian. If he continues to insist on his innocence in the face of certain guilt, continue through the process, not concentrating on his guilt, but telling him about your concern for him in light of his struggle both with the particular area of sin and with his dishonest resistance to acknowledging the struggle. There is some reason why he resists telling the truth—it could be fear of discipline, fear of disapproval or rebellion, to name a few. It is as important to address the dishonesty as it is to correct the behavior that occasioned the lie.

both will repeat itself

If you suspect his guilt, but are not sure, it is better to accept his word. If it is a pattern of behavior, it will surface again. But take the opportunity to tell him why you are concerned. Remind him of the sowing and reaping principle of Scripture. Pray for him, in his presence as well as privately, that God will melt his heart with the truth and that he will choose God's way.

Remind your child of formative instruction. "How did you respond in your heart? How did that dictate your actions?"

"Billy, do you remember what our heavenly Father says about complaining and anger?"

Response

"Complaining and anger come from the heart. Your complaints over breakfast and your shirt expose internal problems, don't they?"

Response

"A complaining spirit shows a thankless, ungrateful heart toward God and others. 2 Timothy 3:2–4 lists ungratefulness with sins of godlessness. Your anger with your sister and returning evil for evil show your heart conflict about whether to love your sister or yourself, don't they?"

Response

"I (we) know what that struggle is like, Billy. I (we) struggle with those sins as well. It is good for us to remember what God says about the dangers of sin and his remedies, his promises, and his help for our struggles."

show God's view on that sin.

Go to Scripture to bring out God's view of the particular area of sin. Remember, whatever struggles with sin are common in your children's daily life should be the regular content of devotional times—not to "rub their nose in it," but to identify it for both children and parents. This *formative instruction* gives you an opportunity to describe sin, its deception, and God's promises to overcome. Then, when *corrective discipline* is called for, you've already covered this territory and disarmed resistance. <u>Your formative instruction laid the foundation for corrective discipline.</u>

Children will acknowledge the truth of God's ways in formative instruction, <u>especially if they have the comfort of you standing with them rather than over them.</u> You can graciously appeal to their previous acknowledgement in corrective discipline. "Remember when we talked about . . . We agreed that . . ."

Remind your child "There are serious outcomes that you are reaping for the sin you have sown. Where was God in this struggle with sin?"

<u>Consider what we reap when we sin.</u> Remember the deeper dimensions of sin we discussed earlier. We reap in relationship to God, in habits for life, in reputation, in relationship with one another, in long-term usefulness in Christ's kingdom, and in eternity. Talk about the spiritual, temporal and eternal benefits of choosing God's ways and the spiritual, temporal and eternal consequences of falling to temptation.

"Billy, where was God this morning?"

Response

"Were you thinking of his warnings and promises when you complained and got angry at Sis?"

Response

"Do you think he knew what was going on in your heart—what your struggles were?"

Response

"Remember <u>Hebrews 4:12–13</u> says:
'For the word of God is living and active. Sharper than any double-edged sword, it penetrates even to dividing soul and spirit, joints and marrow; it judges the thoughts and attitudes of the heart. Nothing in all creation is hidden from God's sight. Everything is uncovered and laid bare before the eyes of him to whom we must give account.'

"Remember, Billy, the consequence of these sins is to harden your heart toward God.

"We have been praying about these particular struggles with sin, haven't we, Billy?"

Response

"Discontentment and anger when someone touches your belongings are especially difficult struggles for you, aren't they?"

Response

"You see, sins we struggle with become habits of life for us. These habits don't magically go away at a certain age. They stick with us. That's why we are talking about this. We want you to overcome these habits now, with God's help, so that they don't follow you through life. That wouldn't be good for you, would it?"

Response

"It is a terrible consequence to carry sinful habits with you through life. Billy, Proverbs 20:11 reminds us, 'Even a child is known by his actions, by whether his conduct is pure and right.' Complaining and anger give you a bad reputation and hurt your relationships with your sister and us. When you are complaining, we do not enjoy the closeness and joy that we want our family to know. And complaining against Mother is disrespectful, isn't it?"

Response

"That interrupts our enjoyment of a normal relationship with you. You feel the breakdown in relationship right now, don't you?"

Response

"Your sister always feels like she has to protect herself from your anger. What do you think your reputation is with her at this moment?"

Response

"You have a reputation with her as an angry, out of control brother. You see, Billy, you are reaping a sad consequence in your reputation and relationships in your family.

"Billy, you often pray for opportunities to be a witness for Christ. Let me suggest that you think about being a witness in our home at breakfast and in your relationship with your sister. Let's ask God to transform the way you think about living for him to include these common experiences of life. That will give you the 'right to speak' and prepare you well for long-term usefulness in Christ's kingdom."

How Can You Help Your Child?

(1) *Identify with your child in the struggle to resist sowing to the flesh.*

Come alongside your child. You know your weakness during temptation and the failures of the sinful nature. What more powerful way to point to help in the Savior than to share how Christ has helped you in your times of temptation. I *don't* mean commiseration with your child to share what's wrong. I *do* mean acknowledgement of your own need and your dependence on Christ.

"Billy, we love you. We want to help you. Mommy and Daddy know what it is like to complain and feel angry when we can't get our way. But God wants us to trust him when things don't turn out the way we wanted. And he has given the Lord Jesus to comfort and help us when we feel discontent and angry. We want to help you with this struggle of complaining and anger when you can't have your way.

"God has promised in 1 Corinthians 10:13, 'No temptation has seized you except what is common to man. And God is faithful; he will not let you be tempted beyond what you can bear. But when you are tempted, he will also provide a way out so that you can stand up under it.' What do you think that means, Billy?"

Response

"God describes the way out in Hebrews 4:14–16, 'Therefore, since we have a great high priest who has gone through the heavens, Jesus the Son of God, let us hold firmly to the faith we profess. For we do not have a high priest who is unable to sympathize with our weaknesses, but we have one who has been tempted in every way, just as we are—yet was without sin. Let us then approach the throne of grace with confidence, so that we may receive mercy and find grace to help us in our time of need.' What do you think it means to approach the throne of grace in prayer, Billy?"

Response

"Billy, we will pray with you and for you. Let's think of what other ways we can help you. Perhaps we should begin a study of Bible characters who struggled with these same sins. That would remind you that you're not alone when you're tempted to be discontented and angry. It would also remind you of the blessings of thankfulness and peacemaking. Can you think of any other ways we can help you, Billy?"

Response

Design help that causes children to know that we understand the nature of their struggle with sin and that we are ready to hunker down in the trenches with them. Work on some means of help for the particular struggle with sin—perhaps accountability, reminders, standards, checklists, Scripture memorization or Bible study. Prayer should always be one of the means. Encourage your child to come to you to pray when the temptation presents itself, for example when he finds that his sister has been touching his possessions. This is not to tattle on Sis, but to remember that his relationship with her is more important than his "stuff." It is harder to mend the hurts and alienation in the relationship damaged by anger. You can both talk to Sis and clear up the problem of her crossing the boundary of propriety over personal belongings.

Christ helped us rather than standing off in the heavens, shouting, "Hey you, down there, get your act together!" He came to earth in flesh and blood, experiencing the same painful realities as his fallen creation. Why? Hebrews 2, especially verses 14–18, tells us:

> Since the children have flesh and blood, he too shared in their humanity so that by his death he might destroy him who holds the power of death—that is, the devil—and free those who all their lives were held in slavery by their fear of death. For surely it is not angels he helps, but Abraham's descendants. For this reason he had to be made like his brothers in every way, in order that he might become a merciful and faithful high priest in service to God, and that he might make atonement for the sins of the people. Because he himself suffered when he was tempted, he is able to help those who are being tempted.

Christ "came alongside" us in his life, death and resurrection. He is our example. He has modeled for us the holy art of laying down our life for others. His identification with us was irresistible! When parents show children the way, they are deeply impressed with Christ's ability to sympathize with their weakness and give real help.

②   *Identify for Them What It Means to Sow to the Spirit*

What should Billy have done when he couldn't find the shirt he "had" to wear that day? What should Billy have said when he found the dreaded shredded wheat in his bowl at the breakfast table? How should Billy have responded when he found evidence that Sis was rifling through his things? What would reflect the beauty of Christ rather than a selfish heart? Draw Billy into the conversation as much as possible as you examine the following verses. His age and attention span will determine how much of this you go over.

"Billy, do you remember God's greatest command to his people?"

Response

"That's right, 'Love the Lord your God with all your mind, heart, soul, and strength, and love your neighbor as yourself.' What do you think that means, Billy?"

Response

"That's right. Let me paraphrase, Billy. Loving God is reflected in thankfulness for all things and service to his kingdom. Loving others is expressed by thankfulness and cooperation with them.

"Billy, here is a positive picture of sowing and reaping for you in your struggle with sin today. It comes from Philippians 2.

"Verses 1 to 3 describe the unity, comfort, and fellowship we have with him because we are God's children."

Response

"There is a lot of sowing going on in verses 1 to 14. Listen carefully. Verse 1 speaks of tenderness and compassion. Verse 2 reminds us to have the same love and purpose as Christ had in his life and death for us. Verse 3 calls us to sow unselfishness and humility. Verse 4 says to plant seeds of concern for the good of others rather than preferring our own best interest." (Let Billy interact with these spiritual qualities as you list them.) "Verses 5 to 11 remind us of Christ's example of all these qualities. They also speak of God's good pleasure in his Son's life and death. Verses 12 and 13 remind us that our obedience is not a result of the power of the law, but rather the force of grace at work in us—that same power that raised Christ from the dead!" (Talk to Billy about God's promise to strengthen us for our struggle against sin, using Ephesians 6 or other passages.) "Verse 14 zeros in on a big item for sowing for you today! 'Do everything without complaining or arguing.'"

"Whew, Billy, all that sowing! But listen to the reaping part of this passage! It is in verses 15 and 16, 'So that you may become blameless and pure, children of God without fault in a crooked and depraved generation, in which you shine like stars in the universe as you hold out the word of life.' That's what we want for you, Billy. We want you to shine like a star in the universe. That's what you want, isn't it?"

Response

"You may not continue to act, talk, and respond in this way.

"Billy, the standard we have set is based on the principles and absolutes of God's Word. It is not negotiable. You know the standards, values and rules of our home, don't you?"

Response

"You know what our expectations are for you, don't you?"

Response

"We expect that you will behave in accordance with these expectations. We are happy to help you comply in every way we can (as we have discussed above)."

Children need a standard that is held up for them with firm but compassionate tenacity. God's law is *the* standard. God expects all people to live in his world according to his law, not just believers. God will judge all who do not. But he extends mercy to those who come to him in faith.

Our culture of "touchy-feely" sentimentality loves the mistaken notion that compassion and love require lowering standards to make them achievable. This is devastating to the very means that God has established to redeem mankind. God's law is consistent with our creation design and compatible with our creation purpose. When we diminish the law to make it "doable" for our children, we remove the necessity of the gospel. We also demean the nobility of purpose embodied in the two tables of the law, "Love the Lord your God with your heart, mind, and strength and your neighbor as yourself."

[handwritten margin note: don't lower the bar]

Think about the symmetry of God's provision for our fallen race! He designed the earth, its creatures and humankind to live in perfect harmony with him and one another. The Fall brought a devastating end to that perfectly glorious existence. But God made provision—*not* by changing the rules and laws by which the universe would operate to accommodate our fallenness—but by sacrificing his Son to redeem all that was destroyed. When we change the standard, we make God's provision unnecessary. It is as if we say, "Well, that won't work. It is too much to ask you to . . . , therefore, just try to do this much. You should be able to do that." In doing this, we take our children away from God, rather than to the cross. Remember, the law is "the schoolmaster that leads to salvation" (KJV).

"In Light of Sowing Your Sin of ___ You Will Reap___"

"Billy, this is the consequence that you will suffer in light of the choices you have made. These consequences only serve to remind you of the grave spiritual consequences we have already described."

This is where parents bring consequences to the discipline process. The consequences we shape, or even natural consequences, do not play a major role in discipline, as you can see. The consequences we describe here serve only to underscore the fact that God cannot be mocked—that our choices, good or bad, generate a harvest, either for our spiritual growth or to our spiritual detriment. <u>We do not depend on consequences to alter behavior. We want to train the heart of the child.</u> In behavior modification, consequences are the means of shaping or manipulating behavior. In biblical correction and discipline, consequences are a means of demonstrating, in a sensory way, the importance of the spiritual consequences that are accruing in relationship to God, to others and to our selves.

It is so important for us to understand these distinctions and teach them to our children. We want them to understand our discipline, and more importantly, God's governance of the world and their lives for his glory and their good.

"Billy, you will need to use your personal savings to replace your sister's mirror to make restitution for breaking her mirror in anger. Do you understand this?"

Response

You may consider having Billy do his own laundry and help with breakfast for a period of time to underscore the work and sacrifice that are made for his benefit every day. This is not for the purpose of punishing him for his failure—but with the goal of bringing to life what does not come naturally to him—a spirit of thanksgiving rather than complaining and faultfinding.

Opportunity for Children to Respond

"Billy, do you understand all we have talked about?"

Response

"Is there anything you would like to add or any way we have misunderstood you?"

Response

"We love you and we always want you to feel free to talk to us about your questions, fears, doubts, joys—anything!"

Response

One of the most destructive aspects of ungodly discipline and correction is the lack of godly dialogue. God has wonderfully provided all the apparatus for meaningful communication with one another. Yet the most life shaping opportunities parents have in their children's lives are often one-sided. Monologue is not godly communication. Long speeches that try to strong-arm our children with arguments, threats, warnings, and predictions will not change their hearts. It will harden their hearts. <u>All of our conversation with our children</u>

should afford them an opportunity to respond—not as peers, but as children interacting with the direction and instruction of parents. We should encourage children to respectfully respond in conversation to help us understand how they are feeling, thinking, processing, understanding, and responding to our direction and inquiries. Often conversation needs refining so that we don't misunderstand one another. We should be sensitive to whether our observations and assessments are fair and true. This can be done in ways that respect parental authority. Has our child been able to get everything out? Have I adequately understood the situation and circumstances? If a child feels misunderstood or treated unfairly, little will be accomplished. We can disarm so much rebellion by defusing resentment and hurt. Give your children a chance to respond in conversation, especially in times of correction.

Prayer

Prayer must always be a part of the discipline process. It may belong at another place in the process—perhaps after the "How Can You Help Your Child?" section, or even in two or more places in the discipline process. Remember that you are a tangible representative of God for your children. Prayer is like helping your child with a school assignment, and then saying, "Now we're going to call your teacher and confirm all that we have been talking about."

Prayer signals to our children that this is for their benefit, not ours. It puts everything in perspective. Praise, acknowledgement of sin and inability, and placing trust and confidence in God, bring all of your correction, discipline, and instruction to a focused conclusion. Summarize all your hopes and concerns for your child in prayer. Model the truth of 1 Corinthians 10:13 and Hebrews 4:14–16 as you take your children with you to the "throne of grace" in prayer.

> "Dear Father in Heaven, I pray for Billy, and for myself today, with David's prayer in Psalm 139. Search Billy's heart, O God, and know his heart. Test him and know his anxious thoughts about people touching his stuff. See if there is any offensive complaining and ungrateful way in him, and lead him in the way everlasting."

A Final Encouragement

We don't shepherd our children to assure that our children will "turn out right." We shepherd our children to be faithful to the work God has given us. Consequences do not serve as power plays to prove our role or power or strength or to put kids in their place for our convenience. They are designed by God to display the reality of God's ultimate rule in the affairs of men and to extend mercy while there is time to repent and trust in God.

Discipline is not an opportunity for us to show our children who is boss or to hand out punishments that will change their behavior. Even when our consequences are appropriate to underscore God's truth and our standards, <u>discipline is *primarily* an opportunity to remind our children of their need to repent and believe in Christ</u>, and the forgiveness and provision available from God through Christ. We are really declaring God's sovereignty and involvement with all he has created, offering relationship with God through Christ. Show them the beauty and goodness of confession to God and others, and warn them of the coming judgment for unbelief.

CHAPTER 14

Communication

I was counseling a father and his fifteen-year-old son. The son was sullen and rebellious. The father was angry and exasperated. I was trying to help the father communicate in godly ways with his son. And I wanted to help the son hear the wisdom of his father—wisdom that was eclipsed by reckless words.

Suddenly the father sprang from his seat, crossed the room, planted himself inches from his startled son's face, and screamed, "I am your father. You are going to listen to me if it's the last thing you do." His son just stared back at him with a look of calculated indifference.

Not all communication breakdowns have this level of drama. In another counseling session I worked with Roger, who was not a shouter. Instead, he exhausted his daughters with monotone lectures in which he droned on and on with dire warnings of their peril. "I am just afraid you will end up like your cousin, Janelle, who is pregnant and strung out on drugs. You are just like her. That's what I have been trying to tell you for the past four hours."

Your Communication Approach is Guided by Your Child Rearing Paradigm

Your paradigm for child rearing will direct your communication strategies. When controlling and constraining behavior are the focus, they will dictate the ways you speak with your children. Harsh words, yelling and scolding are part and parcel of parenting approaches that focus on behavior management. The focus of this book is on parental nurture and discipleship rather than management and control of behavior.

General Approach to Communication

While many passages in the Bible address communication, we are going to look at several from the wisdom literature of the Bible. There are three qualities of communication that we will outline in this chapter—restraint, pleasant words and understanding.

I want to separate the material of this chapter as far as possible from communication *techniques*. Rather, a life of faith and joyful confidence in God is reflected in patterns of communication that are described in the writings of Solomon, the wisest man on earth. When we describe him as wise, we are reminding ourselves that Solomon lived life in joyful, reverent awe of God, for "The fear of the Lord is the beginning of wisdom" (Prov. 9:10). This same truth is expressed in another way in Proverbs 15:33, "The fear of the Lord teaches a man wisdom."

Speaking with restraint to our children, employing pleasant words and delighting to understand them, are not techniques. They reflect wisdom—wisdom that is found in the fear of the Lord. The qualities that will enable you to speak in helpful ways to your children are spiritual.

Restraint

In my youth, "telling it like it is" was the measure of good communication. People prided themselves on unbridled speech. Many of today's generation of parents were raised by parents who were accustomed to "letting it all hang out." In sharp contrast, restraint is a quality of wise speech. Nurturing speech is not thoughtless or impetuous. "A man of knowledge uses words with restraint, and a man of understanding is even-tempered" (Prov. 17:27). Wise people who speak with restraint have taught themselves to hold back, to limit or control what they say. A man of understanding will speak with honesty, frankness and candor, but his words will be framed to benefit those who hear.

Restrained Speech Is Quiet Speech

Ecclesiastes 9:17 reminds us, "The quiet words of the wise are more to be heeded than the shouts of a ruler of fools." There is a power to quiet words that is not present in shouts or screams. I know that is counter-intuitive. You may think that you are heard and your words have more weight if they are shouted, but the opposite is the case. Shouting trivializes words. Shouting puts emotion in the foreground and meaning in the background.

I once had the charge to counsel a mother who was a screamer. Her red-faced shouting spewed out demands and threats to her children. The more she used screaming as her mode of communication, the less her words had weight and authority with her children. In time the children did not even notice that she was speaking to them. Her fear and failure to trust God were the matrix of her shouting (not a general diagnosis of all shouters). We worked on that and she began to trust God more fully and scaled back the shouting. In time her children began to hear her words and actually give them weight.

Restrained Speech Does Not Use Many Words

In Ecclesiastes 6:11, the preacher warns, "The more the words, the less the meaning, and how does that profit anyone?" You can exasperate your child with too many words. Usually long conversations could be summarized in several sentences because people simply repeat themselves. A couple of short conversations are almost always more effective than one long one.

Parents I have counseled who were guilty of wearing their children out were not trying to hurt their kids. They loved them and were alarmed over things they saw in their lives. When their children were younger they had followed through with discipline. But as the children grew older and parents' methods of discipline changed, they began to drag their children through long and exhausting conversations.

Conversations that carry on too long can become mired in sin. "When words are many, sin is not absent, but he who holds his tongue is wise" (Prov. 10:19). Conversations that go on and on will be susceptible to your weaknesses and your children's weaknesses. After you have exhausted yourself by an emotionally draining conversation, you will find yourself saying unguarded and destructive things to your children. Later when you replay the conversation in your mind you will ask, "How did I ever end up there? That's not where I wanted to go with the conversation."

Restrained Speech Thinks First and Speaks Second

"The heart of the righteous weighs its answers, but the mouth of the wicked gushes evil" (Prov. 15:28). The wise man puts his words on the scales to measure their weight. He thinks. He ponders. He asks himself if this is the right thing to say, the best time to say it, the most pleasant way to frame it. The wicked man, in contrast, gushes out evil. For him there is no careful thought, no restraint, no perception of the importance of words that once spoken can never be unspoken. He simply gushes forth with whatever is in his heart.

"Do you see a man who speaks in haste? There is more hope for a fool than for him" (Prov. 29:20). The alarming thing about this statement is that the Proverbs do not hold out much hope for a fool. You may find, as I have, that the temptation to speak in haste without restraint is the greatest when dealing with your children.

Earlier, in the same fifteenth chapter of Proverbs, Solomon encourages careful speech with the observation, "A man finds joy in giving an apt reply—and how good is a timely word" (Prov. 15:23). Words carefully chosen and delivered in a timely manner are a source of great joy. The joy is a blessing both to the speaker and the hearer.

Thinking about restraint in communication leads naturally to our next topic.

(2) Pleasant Words

As noted above, pleasant words are not a communication technique—they are a reflection of the spiritual grace known as the fear of the Lord. "The wise in heart are called discerning, and pleasant words promote instruction" (Prov. 16:21). The wisdom of heart acquired through the fear of the Lord is reflected in speech patterns marked by pleasant words.

Pleasant words promote instruction. Words that are kind and good, words spoken with love and graciousness, promote instruction. Words that are courteous and tactful evoke a good response.

Harsh, loud, demanding and demeaning words do not reflect the gentle confidence of one who delights in joyful, reverent awe of God. They reflect a heart that is fearful, angry, and controlling. Such words make instruction hard to receive.

Your child has two hurdles to surmount if the words he hears are not pleasant words. He must get hold of the truth you are trying to convey, and he must get over the offensive ways in which you are conveying it. In failing to use pleasant words, you are failing to commend wisdom and failing to model for your children the goodness of the fear of the Lord.

Imagine trying to warn a young person about the dangers of companionship with a friend whom you know to be rebellious and unruly. The task of helping your child hear and accede to this warning is challenging enough. This child may lack the maturity and insight to abandon all defenses and receive your warnings. If you add to that obstacle impatience or harshness in your manner of communication, you have built a barricade almost impossible to surmount.

"A wise man's heart guides his mouth, and his lips promote instruction. Pleasant words are a honeycomb, sweet to the soul and healing to the bones" (Prov. 16:23, 24).

Whenever you read of the wise in the Proverbs you must think in more specific terms than garden-variety insight and discernment. You must always equate wisdom with the fear of the Lord, because that is the way the Proverbs describes wisdom. So when you read of the wise man you think of a spiritual quality—wisdom of insight and understanding that is spiritually obtained through the fear of the Lord. Psalm 25:14 says, "The Lord confides in those who fear him; he makes his covenant known to them." So the wise man, the man who has the fear of the Lord, is one who the Lord draws into his confidence; he is one to whom God reveals his covenant.

These spiritual qualities enable a man to guide his mouth in ways that promote instruction. He greases the wheels of instruction through pleasant words. His mouth and his lips are guided by the wisdom of his heart. He knows he cannot simply vent his unhappiness with his child if he wants to promote instruction. He knows that if his words are to bring healing and sweetness to his child they must be pleasant words—words that are like a honeycomb, sweet and healing.

Use pleasant words in your home. When parents are angry and out of control, it doesn't matter how earnest they may be or how accurate in their assessments; they accomplish nothing. They are not speaking in ways that promote instruction. In fact, as they stand there red-faced, yelling at their children, they are convincing their children they are every bit as much a fool as the children think they are at that moment.

Some parents have said to me, "When I am calm and nice I don't get results. But if I get mad and get in their face, they listen." Sadly they are tragically mistaken. The fact that you can frighten a child into submission by a display of rage does not mean they are listening to you. You have simply bullied your child into submission. Your words have not promoted instruction; they have undermined instruction. Eventually such a child will probably square off against his parents, reflecting back to them the same foolishness the parents expressed through their demeaning speech.

Lest you think that is overstated, consider Proverbs 15:2, "The tongue of the wise commends knowledge, but the mouth of the fool gushes folly." The parent who is berating his child is at that moment gushing folly. In contrast, wise people speak in a manner that commends wisdom. Their pleasantness makes the wisdom they share seem all the more sweet and desirable.

No parent who has demeaned their child, saying, "Don't be such a loser—losers hang out with losers," has ever had that child respond by saying, "You are so right, Mom and Dad. Thank you for telling it like it is." The concern about their child's companions may be well placed, but demeaning the child and the child's friends does not commend knowledge.

There are many verses in the book of Proverbs that elaborate on pleasant words. "The mouth of the righteous is a fountain of life, but violence overwhelms the mouth of the wicked" (Prov. 10:11). Think of your words as a fountain. You want the waters of that fountain to be life-giving, pleasant waters, not waters that are brackish and bitter.

Think of your words as a meal for your children to eat. You want to serve them a pleasant, attractive, tasty meal that will nourish them. This is what Proverbs 10:21 describes, "The lips of the righteous nourish many, but fools die for lack of judgment." Ask yourself as you speak with your children, will these words nourish them? You would never think of serving your children dog food, but many parents speak to their children in more unpleasant tones than they would use on the dog.

Proverbs 25:11 uses the simile of an elegant collectible or an exquisite piece of jewelry, "A word aptly spoken is like apples of gold in settings of silver." An apt word is a word that is especially suited to the circumstances. It is a word fitting and appropriate. Solomon says that such carefully crafted words are elegant and beautiful. We should give the same care to create beautiful settings for our words as jewelers meticulously create a setting of gold in silver. Beautiful collectibles are fashioned with thought and our speech too will be pleasant and beautiful with effort and thoughtfulness.

"Words from a wise man's mouth are gracious" (Eccles. 10:12). Recall for the moment what grace is so we can apprehend "gracious words." <u>Grace is God giving us what we do not deserve.</u> God gives the gift of forgiveness and everlasting life to people who deserve his condemnation. Sometimes parents justify ungracious speech by thinking, "This is what this child deserves." The wise parent, in contrast to that thinking, is gracious. <u>This parent imitates God who is gracious,</u> who kindly gives us what we do not deserve—grace. *[handwritten margin note: imitate God by being gracious]*

The Goal of Communication Is Understanding Your Listener

We usually think of good communication skills as the ability to effectively formulate ideas into words. But the finest art of communication is not the ability to express ideas; it is the ability to understand the person with whom one is speaking.

The book of Proverbs speaks to this issue with poignancy. "A fool finds no pleasure in understanding but delights in airing his own opinions" (Prov. 18:2). How many times have you been a fool in conversation? How many conversations with your children have not focused on understanding them and helping them express their thoughts and ideas? If you are like me, sometimes you may not really be interested in their thoughts and ideas; you simply have something to say. Proverbs 18:2 says that is the communication goal of the fool.

There may be times when you are afraid or unwilling to understand the things your children are thinking. Perhaps you do not want to face the difficult issues that true understanding would bring to the surface. Sometimes you may be afraid that if you understood this child better you would have to change some of your expectations and you do not want to change.

I had a fool's conversation one night with my son. I went to his room before bed to speak with him. I had something on my chest that I wanted to express. I, frankly, was not interested in understanding him; I wanted him to understand me. I did not say anything unkind or abusive. When I had finished I told him that I was glad we had this chance to talk together. I prayed for him and headed off to bed.

A few minutes later there was a knock on our bedroom door.

"Dad, are you guys still up?"

"Yes, come in, what's up?"

"Dad, when you left my room you said you were happy we had talked together. I just wanted to mention that I didn't say anything."

"Oh, I'm sorry. I guess I had a good talk, you had a good listen. If I had let you say something, what would you have said?"

"I don't know; I just wanted to tell you that I didn't say anything." There is a subtext here. The subtext is, "If you really want to know what I would have said, you are going to have to pursue me."

I was a fool that night. I could have said everything I wanted to say in the context of asking my son good questions and drawing him out. I could have delighted in understanding him rather than only in airing my own opinions.

Why is that so important?

When you delight in understanding your children you are expressing your love for them. You are saying to them, "I love you enough to care what you think. I love you enough to want to understand you. I love you enough to ask good questions."

Delighting in understanding encourages your son or daughter to communicate. If they know that Mom and Dad are really interested in what they think, they will be far more likely to open up than if they perceive you as disinterested or indifferent. Listening carefully to what your children are saying, and even to what they are not saying, will induce you to frame your words in ways that facilitate conversation. Without understanding, you may speak to an issue they do not even think about and may miss the things most on their minds.

Proverbs 18:13 speaks to this topic with clarity. *"He who answers before listening—that is his folly and his shame."* I read that proverb and think of conversations I regret.

I could see my son coming and I knew what he was going to ask, so I headed him off at the pass. "I know what you're going to ask and the answer is no."

"But, Dad . . . "

"What part of No! do you not understand?"

"But, Dad, I didn't even get a chance to ask my question."

"You don't have to ask your question. I'm your father and I know what you are going to say before you even open your mouth."

I have answered before listening. My children never respond to that by saying, "Dad, it's so great that you are a mind-reader. I am truly the envy of all my friends."

What my children feel at that point is, "I can't get to first base with you. You 'respond' without even hearing what I have to say."

Foolish responses without listening will make your children disinterested in speaking with you. They will take their conversations somewhere else where they can be heard. If your children are saying, you never listen to me, it is because they feel you never listen to them. Slow down and listen.

There is a perceptive insight in Proverbs 20:5. *"The purposes of a man's heart are deep waters, but a man of understanding draws them out."* There is more depth in your children than you might imagine. You observe their shallowness and giddiness and assume they are vacuous, but there are deep waters in your children. Drawing those deep waters out requires patience and great skill.

Margy recently was counseling a young woman. Things were boiling and surging in her that she had not been able to express because her parents had not been skilled in drawing her out. There were deep waters in this young girl. When she was given a homework assignment, she went home and wrote page after page of deep and insightful analysis of herself and her family. Like this young woman, there are deep waters in your children. Drawing them out is a skill that can be acquired.

It requires being sensitive to the right moment. There are times when children are talkative and times when you cannot pry anything from them with a crowbar. A wise parent goes with the moment. Some moments are moments for walking away from conversation and making a pass at it later when the child is more willing to speak. Other moments, when a child is talking, are moments for dropping everything, if possible, to seize the moment and listen.

Unconditional love and acceptance are necessary to make your children feel safe sharing their deepest and most confusing thoughts. You can accept and love your children in your manner and tone even while you are inwardly confused or even grieved by what they are saying. If you become angry or combative your children will conclude you are not really interested in what they think—only in how you want them to think.

Sometimes young people learn that their true thoughts are not really welcomed or desired. They conclude, my father and mother have life scripted and there is no place in their lives for my struggles with making sense of the world. My parents do not have the time or the interest to work through my questions and thoughts about life.

Drawing out the deep waters means learning to ask good questions. Ask questions that deal with attitudes, feelings, and thoughts. A great question opener is, "Help me understand . . ."

Be prepared to facilitate the process of communication for your children. Many times children are helped if you give them some multiple-choice answers to your questions. If your children say, I don't know, or seem to have trouble matching words with thoughts, help them. Using your understanding of human nature and life in the world, present as many possible answers to the question as you can. "Could it be this . . . or that . . . or some other?" Inserting a funny choice or two can help create a non-threatening context for drawing out these deep waters.

The wisdom and strength to remember and employ these ways of communicating is a spiritual grace. Restraint in speaking, pleasant words that promote instruction and the insight to understand the person with whom I am speaking are all spiritual graces that are derived from Christ's grace to me. As I rest in the power of Christ I receive the enabling grace and strength to communicate with my children in these ways. I will not be an anxious person who is trying to force change. I will be a joyful and hopeful person who is resting in Christ's grace and care, filled with awe and reverence for God, and seeking to fulfill my calling.

CHAPTER 15

The Centrality of the Gospel

We were on a camping trip with the high school students from our church. One of the chaperones was also the father of a teen. At one point he became exasperated with the attitudes and behavior of his son. He spent a few minutes giving him instructions about how he was to behave. I could not help overhearing his parting shot to his son to cap off his instructions. "Just do it!" he shouted. "Just do it."

I remember feeling very sad and pondering questions about my own ministry and the view of the Christian life that had been presented from the pulpit. "Just do it." It sounded more like a commercial for athletic footwear than a prescription for how to live the Christian life. It left me wondering how central the gospel is in our parenting practices.

The Gospel Is Central

The gospel was the center of the apostle Paul's entire theology. Remember his words in Romans 1:16–17. "I am not ashamed of the gospel, because it is the power of God for the salvation of everyone who believes . . . For in the gospel a righteousness from God is revealed, a righteousness that is by faith from first to last, just as it is written: 'The righteous will live by faith.'"

We may conclude from this passage that Paul really believed the gospel was for our salvation. But he also believed that the gospel was for Christians. In fact, in verse 15 of this passage, the apostle wrote that he was looking forward to preaching the gospel to the Christians in Rome. "That is why I am so eager to preach the gospel also to you who are at Rome." Paul found joy in the gospel and never moved beyond the gospel because he knew the gospel was the power of God for salvation—including everything from initial calling by grace, to justification, to ultimate glorification. We never move beyond the centrality of the gospel.

In all our nurturing as parents the gospel must be central. It is the only hope for forgiveness. It is the only hope for deep internal change. It is the only hope for power to live. The grace of the gospel is the center of everything for Christian parents.

The fact is that humanity is sick with a disease far more virulent than Spanish flu or leprosy or AIDS. The disease is sin, and we all have it. We are just as bad as the Bible says, "There is no one righteous, not even one; there is no one who understands, no one who seeks God. All have turned away, they have together become worthless; there is no one who does good, not even one" (Rom. 3:10–12). Not only are we all sinners, but "The wages of sin is death" (Rom. 6:23).

God is righteous and holy. He cannot and will not overlook our sin. If we are to escape condemnation and death we need two things. We need forgiveness for our many sins, and we need righteousness in the place of our unrighteousness. We need someone who will stand between us and God—someone who is like us in our humanity, but unlike us in our sinfulness. God, in mercy and amazing grace, sent his only son to earth. This son lived righteously on our behalf so that God's demand for perfect righteousness could be fulfilled. Then he died as an atoning sacrifice so that God's just wrath in response to our sins might be satisfied. The gospel teaches that through faith in Jesus Christ you and I can be fully forgiven and made completely righteous.

"But now a righteousness from God, apart from law, has been made known, to which the Law and the Prophets testify. This righteousness from God comes through faith in Jesus Christ to all who believe. There is no difference, for all have sinned and fall short of the glory of God, and are justified freely by his grace through the redemption that came by Christ Jesus. God presented him as a sacrifice of atonement, through faith in his blood" (Rom. 3:21–25).

That is the gospel. We must stick close to it. We must never move on. There is no moment of any day in which you and I do not need the grace of the gospel. I am writing these things at 8:00 a.m. Already in this day, which is so young, I have sinned. I have failed to

2 needs

love God with heart, mind and strength and to love others as I love myself. We never move on from the gospel.

Helping Children Prize the Gospel

I have had numerous conversations with young parents who expressed the fear of raising young hypocrites. They fear that since they have taught their children appropriate behavior, they will rear well-behaved children who do not sense their need for grace.

Much of what we have written in this book will help you avoid this problem. Hypocrisy is greatest in homes where the emphasis has been on behavior rather than the heart. If the focus of discipline and correction is on ways the behavior has strayed and on how behavior must change, you will miss the heart. That approach makes the problem *what I do*, rather than *what I am*.

[margin note: focus on beh; what I do vs. what I am]

According to the Bible, the problem we have is too profound to be corrected externally. The root problem is not the wrong that we do. It is the source of that wrong—our hearts. The fact that you and I and our children lie and are envious and disobedient indicates that there is something profoundly wrong with our hearts.

Is a man a thief because he steals, or does he steal because he is a thief? Is he a liar because he lies, or does he lie because he is a liar? The Bible's answer is that he steals because he is a thief, he lies because he is a liar, and he disobeys because he is disobedient. "Even from birth the wicked go astray; from the womb they are wayward and speak lies" (Ps. 58:3).

Sometimes someone will ask, "What about addressing the behavior that is wrong and telling a child to do better. Isn't that part of being a good parent?"

The answer, of course, is that addressing the heart does not mean you don't address behavior. But since behavior is heart-driven, I have to speak to behavior in ways that focus on heart change and not simply behavior change.

[margin note: still address the beh; heart vs. behavior]

This truth can help you keep the gospel central in correction and discipline. You must help your children see the hidden heart issues that lie behind their behaviors that are wrong. You will have conversations like this.

[margin note: help them see their heart issues]

"Honey, you know I am concerned that you have lied to me. Telling the truth is something that is very important in human relationships. If you cannot trust me and I cannot trust you we have no glue to hold our relationship together. Do you understand what I am saying?"

"Yes," the child answers, nodding.

"But do you know what concerns me even more?"

"No."

"My deepest concern for you is that you are just like me. We lie because it seems like telling a lie will go better than telling the truth. And we love ourselves more than we love God sometimes. That is why we tell lies.

sin seems better; we love self more than God.

"That is why Jesus came. If all we needed was for someone to tell us what to do, God would have just sent a prophet. The problem we have in our hearts is so great that just knowing what we ought to do is not enough. We need a Savior who has the power to deliver us from our sins."

If you have a precocious child the conversation could take this direction.

"Do you ever tell a lie, Daddy?"

"Well, honey, there are many ways of lying. Sometimes we can tell a lie by making someone think something about us that is not true. So, yes, sometimes Daddy tells a lie. Do you know what I need to do then?"

"What?"

"I need to confess my sin to God. God says he will forgive us (1 Jn. 1:9). I also need to speak to the person I lied to and ask their forgiveness. And I need to think about my heart. Who was I loving more than God when I lied? I need to confess that sin too.

"You know something, honey? I need God every day just as much as you do. I need his forgiveness. I need him to change me on the inside so that I love him more than anything else, and I need his power to love him and others more than I love myself."

Every opportunity to correct your child is an opportunity to confront him with his profound need of forgiveness and grace. If you make behavior the primary thing that is wrong, you will never get to the hope and power of the gospel. And if your children learn how to jump through your hoops they will become little Pharisees, clean on the outside and dirty on the inside.

Specific Needs Addressed by the Gospel

Our children's needs are the same as our own needs. We need cleansing, forgiveness, deep internal transformation and the power to change. These transforming changes are described in Ezekiel 36:25–27. This is an Old Testament seed text for the gospel. When it is compared to Christ's dialogue with Nicodemus (Jn. 3:1–21), one might even conclude this was Jesus' outline when he spoke with this secret follower.

Cleansing

"I will sprinkle clean water on you, and you will be clean" (Ezek. 36:25). Ezekiel begins with our impurity and need for cleansing. We are all sinners; even our best deeds are filthy rags before God.

Ezekiel elaborates on this need for cleansing by identifying two broad areas of life that scream out for cleansing. "I will cleanse you from all your impurities and from all your idols" (Ezek. 36:25).

Our children's thoughts, motives, and actions are impure and show how profoundly they, like us, need cleansing. Impure thoughts are not limited to sexual sin. Any thoughts that are not consumed with loving God with heart, soul, mind and strength are impure thoughts. The only hope for our children and us is the cleansing power of the blood of Jesus Christ.

Our children, like you and me, have enthroned idols in the place of God. We have made the great exchange Romans 1:25 describes. We have worshiped and served created things rather than the Creator. Every particular sin, every point at which I choose to disobey the law of God is due to this great exchange. I am worshiping and serving created things rather than the Creator. All sin problems are worship problems. They have their roots in idolatry.

The worship of idols in our children's hearts cries out with the need for cleansing.

Forgiveness

We and our children also need forgiveness. We cannot change our history. Even if we would never sin again, we still need forgiveness. Our sins are great enough to consign us to eternal damnation. We cannot work our sins off. Though we cannot earn forgiveness, we can receive it as God's free gift of grace. The promise of the new covenant in Jeremiah 31 promises the forgiveness sinners so desperately need. "For I will forgive their wickedness and will remember their sins no more" (Jer. 31:34).

In order to underscore the importance of Christ's perfect life and death on the cross, I used to emphasize for my children that love is not the basis for forgiveness. Instead, forgiveness is based on payment. God's love moved him to send his Son. The Son loved us and gave his life as a ransom. <u>Christ *paid*</u> the penalty for sins and forgiveness is offered on the basis of payment.

Internal change

Since the problem with us is greater than just the things we do, we have a profound need for deep internal change. Ezekiel speaks to this need. "I will give you a new heart" (Ezek. 36:26). The promise of this passage is that grace brings radical internal change. *I will remove from you your heart of stone and give you a heart of flesh.*

We and our children need change that is that radical and thorough. When a child has gained renewed interest in a toy simply because a sibling would like it, that child is exhibiting a stony heart. That hardness of heart will not be melted through anything other than grace. <u>Manipulation of behavior through rewards or punishments will never touch the stony heart</u>. In fact, if you think about it, most behavioristic manipulation makes its appeal to the stoniness of your child's heart. Behaviorism appeals to his compulsive self-love, his pride and his love of pleasure to produce externally appropriate behaviors.

Only grace can change the heart. What encouragement! The very thing that we need is the very focal point of God's work. God gives a new heart—a heart of flesh.

Empowerment

Not only do we need internal change, we need empowerment. If we are to find joy in God and in a self-giving and gracious way of life, we need empowerment. If we are going to turn from idolatry to worship and serve God alone, we need empowerment. <u>It is not enough for us to know what we ought to do.</u> God has promised power to enable us to do it. "I will put my Spirit in you, and move you to follow my decrees and be careful to keep my laws" (Ezek. 36:27).

God cares about more than externally appropriate behavior. He calls us to *love* our neighbor as we love ourselves. While we and our children cannot do that on our own, we have the assurance that God's grace empowers living in extraordinary ways. Paul reminds us, "I can do all things through Christ who gives me strength" (Phil. 4:13).

The fact that Christ gives strength does not mean there is no place for the disciplines of the Christian life. God calls us to strive. He commands that we work out our salvation with fear and trembling, but none of that is possible without God's enablement.

Everything we need from God is here—cleansing, forgiveness, radical internal change and empowerment. The more profoundly our children know the dark and secret caverns of the heart, the more profoundly they will understand their need for grace. If we are going to amaze them with grace, these truths must be before them at all times.

Keeping Grace in Place

Times of correction and discipline are times for nurture and discipleship. Remember that the word *discipline* is closely related to *disciple*. Rather than thinking in terms of crime and punishment, we must think in terms of discipleship and ministry. Discipline is an opportunity to speak of grace.

Grace

Have you ever noticed how much our children are like us? They fail in the same ways again and again. They sometimes grow discouraged by their failures.

One night we were putting our daughter to bed when she began to pour out her unhappiness with life. She felt exasperated with her brother. He had taken advantage of her, but her response was unkind and she knew it. She felt upset over his sin, her sin, and the brokenness of life in a fallen world. It all seemed very crushing to her twelve-year-old heart. She wondered aloud, "Why bother to pray. Why even hope it will be different tomorrow? I never seem to change. He never seems to change either. It's no use; I can't be the person I am supposed to be."

What did she need to hear that night? Did she need some tips about counting to ten when she felt angry with her brother? Did she need for me to tell her that if she really wanted to do better, and tried hard enough, she could? No! No!

What she needed was to be reminded that there is a God who is full of grace and mercy. She can approach his throne of grace and find mercy for past sins and grace for present and even future temptations (Heb. 4:14–16).

We want to highlight for our children the fact that there is a Savior who came to this earth and lived as a sinless man. He took on himself all the suffering and misery of life on this planet. He has all authority and power and is full of grace.

Grace as Motivation

One of the important reasons to emphasize grace is that it is a motive to godliness. As our children see, believe, and embrace the grace of the gospel they are motivated to grow and change. Our task is to hold up before them the goodness, grace, kindness, mercy, and love of God. Their duty to obey God —while vitally important—can only be embraced evangelically in light of the transforming grace and empowerment of the cross.

This is a consistent emphasis in the ministry of the apostles. They use the grace of God as an inducement to follow him:

> Romans 12:1, *Therefore, I urge you, brothers, in view of God's mercy, to offer your bodies as living sacrifices, holy and pleasing to God—this is your spiritual act of worship.* God's mercies are the point of appeal for holiness.

> 2 Corinthians 5:14–15, *For Christ's love compels us, because we are convinced that one died for all, and therefore all died. And he died for all, that those who live should no longer live for themselves but for him who died for them and was raised again.* Seeing Christ's love displayed in his death on the cross motivates the believer to *no longer live for themselves but for him who died for them and was raised again.*

> Titus 3:3–7, *At one time we too were foolish, disobedient, deceived and enslaved by all kinds of passions and pleasures. We lived in malice and envy, being hated and hating one another. But when the kindness and love of God our Savior appeared, he saved us, not because of righteous things we had done, but because of his mercy. He saved us through the washing of rebirth and renewal by the Holy Spirit, whom he poured out on us generously through Jesus Christ our Savior, so that, having been justified by his grace, we might become heirs having the hope of eternal life.*

Help your children to see that the motivation for obedience is the amazing grace of God in the gospel. We were just as bad as everyone else in the world. But then the goodness and mercy of God appeared. Paul expounds the very heart of his theology as follows: Grace Alone, Faith Alone, God's Glory Alone. In Titus 3:8, he adds these signifi-cant words, "This is a trustworthy saying. And I want you to stress these things, so that those who have trusted in God may be careful to devote themselves to doing what is good." Paul is zealous that we emphasize grace. The passage in Titus 3:3–7 serves as a motivation to do what is good.

The chief way the apostles motivated Christians to obey God was to emphasize God's grace, kindness, mercy, love and free forgiveness through the cross. The more that believing children grow in their understanding of the free forgiveness of God and the full righteousness of Christ given to all who embrace Jesus by faith alone, the more they will grow in holiness. The pattern of the apostles is to promote grace-motivated obedience.

The power of the gospel is our hope in this parenting task. We come to parenting with all of our weaknesses and failings. God is not finished with us yet, but we still have this task of teaching our children. We come to him with our profound need for grace and strength to do all the things he has called us to do.

The power of the gospel is not just for our children; it is for us. The power of grace in the gospel will cleanse us, forgive us, change us internally and empower us to be all that we need to be to instruct the hearts of our children. Don't be put off by your needs and weaknesses. Our weakness will never keep us from God as much as our strength will. Come to Christ each day knowing that you can do all things through him who gives you strength.

Notes

1. Terry Johnson, *The Family Worship Book? A Resource Book for Family Devotions* (Fearn, Tain, Ross-Shire, Scotland, UK: Christian Focus, 2003).

2. Tedd Tripp, *Shepherding a Child's Heart* (Wapwallopen, PA: Shepherd Press, 1995), pp. 165–170.

3. Iain Murray, *Jonathan Edwards—A New Biography* (Edinburgh, Scotland: Banner of Truth Trust, 2003), p. 5.

4. Paul David Tripp, *Instruments of Change Workbook* (Philadelphia, PA: Changing Lives Ministries, 2000), pp. 2–3.

5. David Powlison, "Crucial Issues in Contemporary Biblical Counseling," *The Journal of Pastoral Practice* 9, no. 3 (1988): 53–77.

6. Paul David Tripp, *Age of Opportunity* (Phillipsburg, NJ: P&R Publishing, 1997), pp. 128–37.

7. Maurice Roberts, *The Thought of God* (Edinburgh, Scotland: Banner of Truth Trust, 1994), p. 56.

8. "I Am His and He Is Mine," *Hymns of the Christian Life,* (Harrisburg, PA: Christian Publications, 1936).

9. Walter Wangerin, *Ragman and Other Cries of Faith* (New York: Harper Collins, 2004), pp. 23–25.